How To Day Trade From Home: 3-Hour Crash Course

The Beginners Guide to Trading Psychology and Proven Strategies for Success

Edward Day

from various sources. Please consult a licensed professional before attempting any techniques outlined in this book.

By reading this document, the reader agrees that under no circumstances is the author responsible for any losses, direct or indirect, that are incurred as a result of the use of the information contained within this document, including, but not limited to, errors, omissions, or inaccuracies.

Table of Contents

Introduction

"Real wealth is not about money. Real wealth is: not having to go to meetings, not having to spend time with jerks, not being locked into status games, not feeling like you have to say 'yes,' not worrying about others claiming your time and energy. Real wealth is about freedom."
— James Clear

Who honestly wants to spend the rest of their lives chained to a desk, getting berated by a heartless boss while in a constant state of anxiety, just to make ends meet? I know that I certainly didn't and I can't imagine that anyone else does either. Life is short. Why spend your time doing things that you hate in order to make money when you could make your money work for you and spend your time doing the things that you love with the people that you love?

What if I told you that, regardless of your current financial status, you too could become a millionaire and spend the rest of your life traveling the world on your own private yacht, sipping fruity cocktails, and lounging about in the sun? Well, it's the truth. Let me tell you how.

Who I Am

I'm not preaching from a pedestal; I used to be just like you. I'm a family man with simple interests. I love fishing (who doesn't?) and I'm at my happiest when I'm walking my dogs. I was just your average guy trying to get by, but I wanted to be able to offer my wife and daughters more. I think every father wants to be able to lay the world at his children's feet, and I was no different. I followed all of the golden rules that parents and teachers give us, promising us that we'll be successful if we manage to abide by them. I was a good student, enough so that I went off to earn bachelors' degrees in finance and accounting after high school. A lot of people are put off of studying degrees that involve dreaded numbers, but I went ahead and did it because I wanted to be financially successful. I've always loved business and finance, so it was an easy pill to swallow. In order to make sure that I'd be extra successful I went off and completed an additional bachelor's degree in economics as well as completing my master's in accounting. However, all of the education in the world couldn't have possibly prepared me for what came next.

My life was on track to being the magical shower of financial success that society guarantees those of us who "throw our backs into it." I had numerous degrees and soon started working as an accountant. I thought *"this is it, this is really it—this is how I'll get my financial freedom and secure my family's future."* But it wasn't. I enjoyed my job, but I didn't enjoy the monotony of the nine-to-five lifestyle that I was living, I didn't enjoy being away from my family all of the time, and I soon came to realize that while the pay wasn't bad, I'd never become a millionaire from that paycheck alone. I knew then that I had been bamboozled, just like so many before me, into believing that hard work alone was enough to help you to reach financial freedom. It isn't. I wanted to break free, but I didn't know how. That is, until 2008 rolled around and turned my life upside down. In the blink of an eye, I reevaluated my entire life and decided to head down a different road, the one less traveled by.

Just a little over twelve years ago I was working as an accountant for a client who made all of his money off of forex trading, and he made a lot of it, which means that I was instantly intrigued. We soon became firm friends and before I knew it I was accompanying him to a seminar on that very subject. I was hooked immediately and knew that forex trading would be my gateway to the lifestyle I had always dreamed about. It wasn't long before I realized that I had a knack for it. I handed my letter of resignation to my boss, packed up my office, walked out of the door with nothing but a dream in my heart, and never looked back. Switching to being a full-time forex trader was honestly the best decision that I ever made, albeit the scariest too. Most of us throw our dreams away because we'd rather settle for certain mediocrity than uncertain success, but I didn't want to spend the rest of my life counting my cents and chasing dollars. If reaching for success wasn't scary, everybody would do it and every second Tom, Dick, or Harry would be the new Bill Gates. Being willing to take risks is one of the key characteristics that you need to embody if you want to join America's wealthiest one percent. You need to be willing to walk the path less traveled, like me, if you want to get to places that most other people never get to.

Where am I now? Well, I'm sitting pretty. I have a few mentees of my own now, people whom I'm trying to help to become financially successful too. I'd like to help you put your bank account on steroids too, if you're willing to accept my assistance. I've made quite a bit of money off of forex trading, and although I don't like to brag, I can say that it's more than enough to insure that my two daughters, my wife, and I will always have enough money to live comfortably. I've been privileged enough to have been invited to a number of stock trading and forex seminars as a speaker to share my knowledge over the years too. Sharing what I've learned is one of my greatest passions. I feel somewhat responsible for "paying forward" the knowledge that my own mentors imparted on me. I've received so much guidance and help from so many businessmen and women who were in no way obligated to help me that I feel that I should do the same for others. In fact, I feel compelled to do the same for you.

Who You Are

Believe it or not, I can probably hedge a pretty good bet on the kind of person you are. It's nothing to be embarrassed about or anything to take offense over, it's simply a matter of fact that there is generally a special "kind" of person who becomes interested in the kind of profits that day trading offers.

Just like me, you're likely someone who has spent most of your life working a normal job, but you're probably not experiencing the kind of financial freedom you were hoping to experience, you work forty (or more) hours a week yet the bills just keep piling up, and things seem to be getting more expensive every year while your salary just never seems to change. If that's you right now, you are where most other billionaires were when they decided to turn their lives around and make a change too.

Change needs a catalyst, however, just like a fire needs a spark. If you've picked up this specific book, there's probably something pushing you to change. Maybe your financial position has changed, your significant other has lost their job, you've found out that you're pregnant (or that your significant other is expecting), you've gotten engaged, you've bought a house, or you've decided to leave your current employment—whatever it may be, you can draw some comfort from the knowledge that these factors were major parts in many self-made millionaires' journeys to success. If we were all perfectly content with our circumstances or if we all felt entirely secure in our lifestyles, we would never feel motivated to change.

Regardless of what inspired you to choose this particular book, I'd like you to know that this is the start of our very own shared journey. A journey during which I will take your hand, just like my mentors took mine, and guide you through the basics and intricacies of day trading. I'm here to help you to make that change you've been dreaming about.

Why You Can Become a Billionaire (or Settle for Being a Millionaire)

A lot of people don't even want to try to become wealthy because they've been indoctrinated into thinking that they'll never escape the middle class no matter what they do, and it's an absolute pity because nobody's fate is written in the stars. If you want to be a millionaire, you can be a millionaire—heck, you could even be a billionaire. It's not that hard, but it does require a good bit of grit and determination, but you have that—don't you? I'm sure you do because if you didn't you wouldn't have gone through the effort of picking up a book on day trading with the intention of fully committing to it.

Do you know how many millionaires there are living in the United States of America right now? Eleven million. Eleven million is a substantial number. You're ten times more likely to become a millionaire in America than you are to catch the human immunodeficiency virus (also known as HIV). A lot of people have worried about the dangers of contracting HIV at some point in their lives (most likely during health class in high school), but have you ever worried about how you'll spend your money when you have too much of it to know what to do with it all? Of course you haven't because we're intrinsically wired to worry about the worst-case scenario without even considering the best-case scenario. This is the kind of mindset that I'm going to be challenging in this book. It's time that you step out of your old tired ruts and realize that you're just as deserving of "the good life" as Mark Zuckerberg, Elon Musk, or Bill Gates is. There's absolutely no reason why your bank account shouldn't reflect a six-figure number too.

A lot of modern millionaires and billionaires made their money on the stock market and a good portion of them did it while day trading. Have you heard about a guy named George Soros? Soros was born in Hungary in 1930. By the time he was a teenager, Europe was in the midst of the worst war it had ever seen and he and his parents fled to Britain. He has told some harrowing stories about this time period, that saw his Jewish neighbors torn away from their homes and shipped off to concentration camps, during interviews. Despite having lived through one of the worst time periods in human history, Soros decided that he wanted to make a success of his life.

He started getting involved in forex day trading (buying and selling foreign currencies) when he was about 26 years old and set up his own hedge fund at 43. Initially he allowed members of the public to invest in his hedge fund, essentially starting trading with it at a balance of

$12 million. He soon turned this $12 million that his clients had entrusted him with into $25 billion and proved that his active trading strategies were as effective as they were easy to understand. He made the bulk of his personal fortune off of short selling the British Pound. He did this by "borrowing" British Pounds from a stockbroker only to sell them for an immense profit after their value crashed when Britain entered the European Union. This crash largely occurred because the British government had artificially increased its currency's value but failed to maintain this faux increase. Today Soros is worth more than $8 billion, a figure that doesn't accurately reflect the amount of money he has made during his lifetime because he has given most of it away to his chosen charities over the years.

Soros isn't the only person to have made some serious cash while day trading either. Soros mentored a guy called Stanley Druckenmiller, who made billions off of it too. Druckenmiller has been managing millions (if not billions) of dollars belonging to clients through his investment fund called Duquesne Capital for decades (although he retired and closed it in 2010). Druckenmiller managed to acquire about $5 billion in personal wealth during his years as a day trader (so I guess we can be pretty sure that he's not too concerned about funding his retirement).

Both Soros and Druckenmiller are past retirement age, but having been born in the mid-1900s isn't a requirement for becoming a day trading millionaire. There are some youngsters making millions out there too. Tim Grittani started day trading with $1,500 to his name (a sum of money that had been given to him during his bar mitzvah) at the age of 23. He followed some of the tips of short courses offered by Timothy Sykes online and within a year he managed to turn his humble start-up capital into $128,000. A year later reports state that he's made more than $1 million (all while still in his early twenties). What makes Grittani even more exceptional is the fact that almost all of his money has been made off of day trading penny stocks. Penny stocks are the cheapest stocks around; this means that you need to trade an incredibly large volume of them in order to make a substantial profit.

Your surname doesn't need to be Soros, Druckenmiller, or Gritanni in order to make a humble (or huge) profit off of day trading. All you need is the determination to follow your dreams and you've already proved that you have that by picking up this book.

Why This Book Is About To Change Your Life

I'm about to change your life and I don't say that lightly. Once you reach the last period on the last page of this book, it's entirely possible that you won't even be able to recognize the person you are right now. I'm going to make it possible for you to take those exotic vacations you've always dreamed about going on, to send your children to private schools, to pay off the mortgage on your house, to purchase that car you've only ever drooled over on *Top Gear*, and to quit your day job. If your daughter comes to you and asks for a pony, you'll be able to get one for her. Heck, you'll be able to get her the whole barn, and why shouldn't you? We all deserve to be able to live that kind of lifestyle and it's entirely within your reach.

Over the next six chapters I'm going to:

- Define day trading;
- Discuss the day trading rule;
- Define day trading's terms and jargon;
- Tell you the kind of person that is best suited to day trading (and how to become just like them);
- Describe the kinds of commodities that can be traded using day trading (including forex, commodities, stocks, cryptocurrencies, futures, and binary options);
- Define the most popular day trading strategies (scalping, range trading, news based trading, and high frequency trading);
- Tell you about the risks associated with day trading;
- Tell you about the kind of profits that you can expect to make from day trading;
- Discuss the psychological toll of day trading;

- Talk about how to handle commission fees and taxes so that they do not cut into your profits too much;
- Tell you what market fluctuations are and why they occur;
- Teach you how to read the market;
- Discuss the importance of starting off with a demo-account (as well as defining what a demo-account is and discussing which one is the best fit for you);
- Talk about brokers (who they are, what they do, which brokers are the best, and which brokerage firm would be best suited to you);
- Discuss day trading without a broker with the use of software like *Ally*;
- Note the value of online courses pertaining to day trading (many of which are free); and
- Give you tips and tricks for maintaining the right kind of mindset to be successful in day trading.

Most importantly, I'm going to give you step-by-step instructions on how to get started, which is absolutely the scariest part of the whole experience.

Chapter 1:

What Is Day Trading?

Day trading might sound like the perfect way to play the stock market and to avoid vampires at the same time, but it's a bit more complicated than that.

Day trading is a type of stock trading. Stock trading involves buying and selling stocks on the stock market with the aim of making a profit. Stocks are little "pieces" of businesses that publicly traded companies make available for sale in order to raise capital to continue or expand their operations. These pieces sell for lower or higher amounts depending on the size of the company that issued them and its profitability or performance over the past fiscal year.

Some kinds of stocks, like preferred stocks, entitle you to a portion of the company's profits. This portion is called a dividend. Other stocks, like common stocks, give you voting rights when it comes to selecting the company's board members and in making operational decisions.

Stock trading has been a part of society for hundreds of years. The first stock exchange ever founded was created in Amsterdam by the Dutch East India

Company in 1611. They founded it in order to facilitate the sale of "portions" of their voyages. This point in history saw a number of their ships besieged by pirates; this meant that singular investors were hesitant to bet on funding an entire voyage but were more open to taking the risk of investing in a portion of the voyage's costs with the promise of receiving a proportional piece of its profits should it be successful. Selling portions of a voyage was therefore an early form of investment diversification.

It wasn't long before it spread to the New World too. In 1790 the United States of America saw the birth of its very own first stock exchange in the form of the Philadelphia Board of Brokers. It was originally formed (in a caffeine-driven frenzy, I'm sure) in an upmarket coffee house on Philadelphia's Walnut Street and within approximately 100 years it was dealing in nearly $400,000 worth of stocks. By 1875 it was officially known as the Philadelphia Stock Exchange. Despite having been the first it was certainly not the most influential. This honor goes to the New York Stock Exchange (or else that movie starring Leonardo DiCaprio might have been called *The Wolf of Walnut Street*).

The New York Stock Exchange (also called "the NYSE" and "The Big Board") was founded two years after the Philadelphia Board of Brokers was created. It was born out of the convictions of two dozen traders who met under a buttonwood tree to sign the agreement (known as the Buttonwood Agreement) that defined its ambitions and operational goals. It has since grown to be the largest stock exchange in the world, facilitating the trade of more than $170 billion worth of stocks every single day.

The Definition of Day Trading

As I said earlier, day trading is a type of stock trading, but it's a very special kind of stock trading because it allows you the opportunity to make a lot more money than you would be able to if you utilized more traditional methods. Have you ever received an email from a Nigerian prince promising you $1,000,000 if you're willing to pay him the transfer cost of $10,000? Well, day trading is like that—except it's real.

Day traders are people who buy a bunch of stocks at the beginning of the trading day, only to sell all of them again before the end of the trading day. When a day trader successfully buys a number of stocks from a certain company and then sells them again during the same trading day it is known as a "round trip." Professional day traders execute tens (if not hundreds) of round trips every single day. Most traditional stock trading strategies involve holding on to stocks for up to 15 years. Yet imagine how much more money you could make if you were making hundreds of small profits every day instead of waiting nearly two decades to see a profit.

Day trading is more difficult than most other traditional stock trading methods, though, because it requires that you have a keen insight into the stock market's future projections as well as a natural intuition for making good trades. A good day trader just instinctively knows when to buy and when to sell, although honing this ability can take years and years of practice and dedication (until then you can refer back to this book for guidance).

Day traders make money by buying stocks that they expect to increase in value within a couple of hours before their price starts increasing and selling them once their prices have peaked a few hours later. These short-term increases in stock prices are normally caused by market sentiment rather than by market performance. This means that successful day traders need to be in tune with your average investor in order to predict whether a certain stock will be bullish or bearish on any given day.

For most of day trading's history it has only been defined by those who practiced it, but in 2001 the Financial Industry Regulatory Authority (abbreviated as FINRA) decided to define and regulate it under *Pattern Day Trader Rule 4210*. They didn't decide to do this to give day traders a sense of community but in an attempt to deter investors from making use of this trading strategy at all. Of course they've stated that the restrictions that they've placed on traders is for their own financial protection, citing studies showing that many day traders lose money while day trading, but it could be argued that they'd simply like to limit the amount of millionaires and billionaires created by the stock market.

Pattern Day Trader Rule 4210 states that anyone who has less than $25,000 in their trading account is not allowed to make more than three round trip trades in 120 hours (or five consecutive days). Your trading account could be frozen for nearly three months if you're caught contravening this rule. However you are allowed to make an unlimited amount of roundtrips if you have more than $25,000 in your trading account.

You need to be able to buy a large number of stocks at once in order to make enough money off of day trading to live on. Traders would say that you need to maintain a high trade volume because you'll likely make only a couple of cents' profit on every share sold. You'd only make about $30 in profit if you sold 100 shares at a profit of $0.30 per share, but you'd make $30,000 if you sold 100,000 at the same profit margin. Most day traders buy on margin to be able to pull off such immensely large trades and you need a special kind of trading account (called a margin account) to do so. Many (if not all) brokers and brokerage firms require that you deposit at least $2,000 before they're willing to open a margin account on your behalf. When you're buying on margin you're essentially borrowing money (with interest) from a stockbroker or brokerage firm in order to make up for a shortfall in your funds—all so you can acquire a certain number of stocks belonging to a specific company.

Most margin accounts allow you to borrow up to half of the sale price of the lot of stocks you're looking to purchase. Any money that you make once you begin selling some of these stocks goes directly to the broker or brokerage firm that lent you the money to make the purchase, until the sum is repaid (with interest) in full. Brokers and brokerage firms also normally require that you keep a certain amount of cash in your account at all times. If you don't, they'll force you to make a "margin call." When they force you to make a margin call, they essentially force you to sell some of your stocks until your account contains the minimum amount of money it requires to remain open. Alternatively, they'll give you the chance to personally deposit funds into it to top it up if you have enough money at your disposal to do so.

The problem with buying on margin is that it is incredibly risky because even if you continuously make profits on the sale of the stocks held within your margin account, you will still be required to pay back the money that was lent to you and the interest that its loan has accrued in the meantime. For this reason, and this reason alone, you shouldn't even consider opening a margin account until you have a couple of successful years of day trading behind you. Going into debt that you wouldn't be able to repay with your personal funds is an incredibly risky game that should only be left to the professionals (and to those who are willing to risk total bankruptcy).

If you're just starting out, I highly recommend that you only trade with your own money even if it means that your profit margin may be a bit smaller in the beginning.

Day trading is a legitimate career option for those who are willing to put in the time and the effort. Sure, you may have to spend a couple of hours reading books and watching videos in order to learn how to do it well, but you might make billions in the process—so I'd say that it is worth it.

The History Of Day Trading

Stock trading may have started more than 300 years ago, but it took us another 150 years to invent trading. It wasn't that our forefathers weren't creative or industrious enough to invent it, it's just that it physically wasn't possible up until that point. Why? you might ask. Well, it has to do with the invention of ticker tape in 1867. Ticker tape was the very first way that stock exchanges (and thus stock prices) could be communicated across stock exchanges in real time. It made use of telegraph lines to produce a long strip of paper from a "stock ticker." This piece of paper contained information on how many stocks belonging to a certain company were sold and for what prices, tagging this information with an abbreviated form of the company's name in order to make it recognizable.

Before the invention of ticker tape this information could only be shared between stock traders and stockbrokers through handwritten messages on little pieces of paper. This meant that it couldn't be shared between states and that it was usually outdated by the time that it was received by its intended recipient. The inaccuracy in stock price and trading volume reporting back in those days meant that traders simply couldn't day trade because they didn't have enough information on the stocks' prices in order to be able to exploit small fluctuations in them. Of course (and luckily for us) all of this changed when traders realized that they could keep abreast of stocks' prices at all times with the use of ticker tape.

The advent of ticker tape made it possible for stockbrokers to day trade, but it was still entirely impossible for stock traders to do so unassisted. This is because traders were not allowed to buy or sell stocks without the aid of a stockbroker until the mid-nineteenth century. While I'm sure that the stockbrokers of the time didn't have any problems with this arrangement, it meant that your Average Joe was completely excluded from being able to make a career out of day trading.

From there on out thousands of normal people started day trading in the shadows, making small (inexplicable) fortunes that confused and frazzled their neighbors and family members—that is, until the chairman of the SEC, Arthur Levitt, defined the practice during a congressional meeting in 1999. At the time he said that he believed that upwards of 7,000 private individuals were involved in day trading in the United States of America at any given time and he certainly didn't approve. Your average American shared his sentiments at the time and you could hardly blame them. In June of that year a full-time day trader named Mark Barton went off on a horrific killing spree that saw him bludgeon his wife, his son (aged 12), and his daughter (aged 10) to death before embarking on a mass shooting at a day trading office, a rampage that cost 12 people their lives and injured an additional 13. This killing spree saw Barton turn the gun on himself before police had the chance to apprehend him, but he did leave a detailed note explaining his motivations. Barton had lost more than $100,000 while day trading in the month leading up to his suicide and blamed his fellow day traders for his losses. The American public saw these murders and Barton's suicide as a sign that day trading was too stressful for any person to bear, leading them to be rather disparaging of it, to say the least. This viewpoint was backed up by a study that was published by the North American Securities Administrators Association mere weeks after Barton's suicide. It stated that ten percent of all day traders went bankrupt from day trading. It's clear that as recently as 20 years ago the government was actively trying to discourage stock traders from making use of day trading although it is now clear that their reasoning for opposing it was erroneous (raising questions regarding their motivations).

Day trading suffered another blow just a year later when the stock market crashed during the recession of 2000. Reckless lending was implicated as one of the reasons for the crash, and suddenly all eyes were on major investors who had day traded using margin accounts (many of whom really did lose everything because of the recession).

Since the year 2000, day trading has slowly started growing in popularity again, and this time it is fully regulated and entirely respected as a profession in its own right. It is expected to continue growing in popularity as more and more people start realizing that they don't need to submit to a tyrannical employer in order to make enough money to live very comfortably. Luckily you've picked up this book early enough to be one of the first to ride the revolutionary wave of financial freedom that is sweeping the nation.

The Different Types of Assets in Day Trading

Day traders haven't limited themselves to traditional stocks alone; they've branched out into investing in a number of different kinds of assets. The most popular of these are cryptocurrencies, binary options, commodities, forex, and futures.

Cryptocurrencies

Cryptocurrencies are a form of decentralized electronic money. They're called decentralized because instead of being "created" by a government's treasury or minting operations, they're created by the internet itself through a process called "blockchain." A cryptocurrency researcher named Jan Lansky compiled a list of six traits that he believes are characteristic of cryptocurrencies. These are: that they don't have central authorities, that they allow changes of ownership to be registered, that their systems can't register more than one change of ownership at a time, that they keep records of the amount of units they have and who owns them, that their systems allow for the creation of new units, and that they allow their users to prove which units (and how many of them) that they own. The most famous cryptocurrency and the one you've probably heard the most about is called Bitcoin.

The first ever cryptocurrency, Ecash, was created by an American computer scientist named David Chaum in 1983. Chaum was way ahead of his time, and despite inventing a software system that would allow you to withdraw this cryptocurrency as cash, his ideas soon fell by the wayside and were forgotten. They remained outside the collective conscience until 13 years later when the USA's National Security Agency (NSA) published a paper on developing cryptocurrency models that was largely replicated a year later and published in *The American Law Review*.

The early 2000s saw the creation of a type of cryptocurrency known as e-gold. This cryptocurrency's holding company bought gold pieces and jewelry made out of gold from their clients in exchange for e-gold units. These units were supposed to be equal in value to the weight of gold that they represented. Owning e-gold units allowed people to trade them (receiving goods or services in return for them), exchange them for their dollar value, or to swap them for their value in actual gold from the company's coffers. Unfortunately e-gold was plagued by the same problem that caused the downfall of so many preliminary cryptocurrencies before it—it found itself being used for dubious purposes like money laundering and as the main currency in a number of ponzi schemes. Not only was it utilized by the criminal underground, it was being targeted by it too. Thousands of e-gold users found themselves targeted by malevolent hackers and phishers that collectively robbed them of millions of dollars' worth of e-gold units over a period of months. Legal pressure, as well as public scrutiny, eventually led to e-gold closing its doors (and recalling all of its cryptocurrency units) for good.

The first modern cryptocurrency was launched in 2009 and it's the one that we all know and love: Bitcoin. Nobody really knows who created it, but we do know that it's a person, group, entity, or organization that calls itself Satoshi Nakamoto. Within two years of its inception, a number of businesses like Microsoft, Newegg.com, WordPress, and Expedia started allowing payments on their platforms via Bitcoin. Bitcoin has managed to grow exponentially in value since then and now trades for about $9,669 per unit.

Of course, Bitcoin isn't the only cryptocurrency that's currently doing the rounds. Ether, Litecoin, XRP, Tether, and Monero are all quite popular too.

Ethereum creates the cryptocurrency called ether as payment for the people that run its "nodes." These nodes are central to the functioning of ethereum as a whole. You see, ethereum was created to not only decentralize its own currency but to decentralize the entire internet. Before ethereum there were only two people that knew your login details to any given site or financial server: you and the person who ran the site itself. Ethereum sought to change this number to one by empowering its users to store information and currency in "nodes" to which no-one knows the login details except for the user themself. This type of encryption also means that it is basically impossible for hackers or phishers to access their users' funds or information. One ether is currently worth about $238.

Litecoin was created by Charlie Lee in 2011 and is the most similar to Bitcoin, as it was specifically created to enable its users to transfer funds to one another in minutes with the added benefit of basically zero transfer costs or fees. Litecoin's transfer time is actually even faster than that of Bitcoin, allowing its users to send money to each other within two and a half minutes from the send action being activated to reception. It is also easier to "mine" (create) Litecoin units than it is to mine Bitcoin units because in order to mine Bitcoin you need a computer set up with an immense amount of processing power while you only need some spare memory on your desktop in order to be able to mine Litecoin units. One Litecoin unit is currently worth about $47.

Ripple created a kind of cryptocurrency called XRP. Ripple itself is a platform that is used by a number of traders and financial institutions to facilitate sales and payments. It is a bit like the Amazon of the crypto-networks because it allows its users to enter what they're looking to trade in exchange for XRP. Unlike Bitcoin and Litecoin, you can't mine XRP units and there were only a limited amount of them ever made (about 1,000,000). It is also different from Litecoin and Bitcoin in the sense that setting up a Ripple wallet to hold your XRP units isn't free; you need to deposit the value of at least 20 XRP units in order to open it. A single XRP unit is currently worth approximately $0.20.

This means that you need to deposit at least $4 in order to open a Ripple wallet.

Tether is a type of cryptocurrency that was created by Tether Limited in 2015. It was created with the intention of basing its value on the US dollar. This characteristic gave rise to the term "stablecoin." A stablecoin is a cryptocurrency that's inherent value doesn't change regardless of fluctuations in the cryptocurrency market, a definition that suits Tether perfectly. It is mainly used as the cryptocurrency with which all other cryptocurrencies are bought or traded for. Currently one Tether unit is trading for about $1.03.

Monero is a type of cryptocurrency that was created in 2014. It is best known for two of its main features: the anonymity it guarantees its users and how easy it is to mine. Monero encrypts and hides all of the information pertaining to recipients, amounts sent, and senders, meaning that transactions made with it are entirely untraceable. This has made it a popular option for rich investors who would prefer that the public not know how they spend their money. However you don't need to be a rich investor in order to be able to afford mining Monero. You don't need a fancy setup or a high-capacity computer in order to mine it. In fact you could probably use your laptop to do it. This means that creating it out of thin air is a real option, even for your Average Joe (when has earning money ever been *that* easy?). One Monero unit is currently worth about $68.

You can day trade cryptocurrencies by buying highly volatile units just before they experience a price increase and selling them once they have experienced that increase. An example of day trading a cryptocurrency would be if you heard that Amazon was about to start allowing payments made in Monero units. A smart day trader would then buy up as many Monero units as they could afford. Let's say that you managed to buy 10,000 Monero units at an initial cost of $68 per unit for a total price of $680,000 just before the news about Amazon started affecting its price. If, once the news broke, a Monero unit's cost rose to $70 and you then sold all 10,000 units you had originally purchased, you would make a profit of $20,000.

Cryptocurrencies are traded on online platforms called cryptocurrency exchanges. These exchanges generally allow their users to trade dollars for cryptocurrencies, as well as cryptocurrencies for other cryptocurrencies. Of course, not all exchanges were created equally and not all of them have the same amount of variety. You should make use of an exchange with as much variety as possible if you're planning on day trading cryptocurrencies.

There are a number of cryptocurrency exchanges that are viable options for day traders, namely Binance, Bybit, ChangeNow, Cex, and Coinbase.

Binance was created by a Chinese-Canadian business executive named Changpeng Zao in 2017 and by 2018 it was the largest cryptocurrency exchange in the world (and by far the most popular among day traders). You can trade a wide variety of cryptocurrencies using Binance like ATOM, Bitcoin, NEO, Ethereum, Ravencoin, XRP, Chainlink, Litecoin, Binance Coin, Tether, and Bitcoin cash. Just after its inception you couldn't use dollars to purchase the cryptocurrencies that it featured, and this proved a problem for start-up cryptocurrency day traders because many of them didn't have any cryptocurrencies pre-purchased to start trading with. Luckily the system has recently changed and now allows for the purchase of cryptocurrencies using dollars or euros.

Bybit is also a favorite amongst day traders but for different reasons. This exchange allows its users to set limit orders, market orders, stop limit orders, stop market orders, fill or kill orders, good till canceled orders, immediate or cancel orders, close on trigger orders, and other conditional orders, and to trade perpetual contracts. It hosts four main cryptocurrencies, namely Ripple's XRP, Bitcoin, Ethereum, and EOS. Bybit is also world-renowned for its customer service, offering users the opportunity to chat with customer service at any hour of the day in the language of their choosing.

ChangeNow is one of the only cryptocurrency exchanges that doesn't require you to create an account with them in order to start trading. It was founded in 2017 and launched its own currency, Bitcoin Gold, at the same time. Not only does it offer its users ease of access and relative anonymity, but it also allows its users to buy, sell, and swap more than 160 different types of cryptocurrencies. ChangeNow also has a fantastic mobile application on which its users can make an unlimited amount of transactions that are essentially guaranteed to be processed in a matter of minutes.

Cex (also often referred to as Cex.io) is one of the oldest cryptocurrency exchanges in the world. Being one of the oldest, we can only assume that it has ironed out most of the hiccups that newer cryptocurrency exchange platforms are prone to experiencing. It was founded in 2013 and was originally meant to function only as a Bitcoin exchange platform. It made the switch to being a full-time cryptocurrency platform in the beginning of 2015 after it closed down its Bitcoin mining operations for good. Unfortunately it offers its users less privacy and anonymity than cryptocurrency exchanges like ChangeNow do because it conforms to US financial security standards by enforcing anti-money laundering policies that require it to verify the identities of its users before allowing them to make any transactions. Cex also offers its users access to its brokerage services for an additional fee. One of Cex's seasoned employees will trade cryptocurrencies on your behalf if you choose to make use of these services.

Coinbase is a cryptocurrency exchange that has more than 30 million users worldwide. Despite its relative popularity, there are some downsides to using it, like strict limits that are placed on the amount of cryptocurrency that you can purchase every day. It limits its dollar-paying users to $50,000 worth of purchases each day and its euro-paying users to €30,000. Of course these limits are high enough that they shouldn't bother or hinder your average day trader too much. It is also one of the slower cryptocurrency exchange platforms and transactions can take up to five business days to complete whereas many other exchanges are capable of completing transactions within minutes. Coinbase can be used to buy, sell, or trade Algorand, Bitcoin Cash, Bitcoin SV, Dai, ATOM, Basic Attention Token, Bitcoin, Dash, Ethereum, Litecoin, OmiseGO, Orchid, Augur, and Zcash.

Creating an account with a cryptocurrency exchange platform is usually as easy as going to its website and clicking on the "create account" or "start trading" buttons. This ease of access means that day trading cryptocurrency is accessible to nearly everyone.

Day traders who make use of cryptocurrency as their main day trading asset use a number of different techniques to decide which cryptocurrencies to invest in. Some make use of technical analysis by trying to identify patterns in the cryptocurrency's price movements over a specific period of time while others keep an eye on the news to try and determine what the market sentiment towards a specific cryptocurrency is. Other day traders feel that they can determine how a certain cryptocurrency is doing by comparing the amount of accounts held with the platform to the actual number of accounts that are truly active on the platform. All three of these methods are credible and reliable, meaning that it's up to you to decide which one you'd like to utilize.

Binary Options

Binary options are a whole other kettle of fish. A binary option is a bit like a bet that you make against the binary broker that offers it. The outcome of this bet either sees you receiving a payout or not—there is no middle ground. An example of a binary option would be if your binary broker offers you a binary option at 60% on whether or not Apple's share price will reach $320 per share by the end of the trading day. If you put down $10,000 on this binary option and Apple's stock price does reach $320 by the end of the day then you receive your $10,000 back as well as $6,000 (60% of $10,000) as a payout, but if it doesn't reach $320 per share by the end of the day, then you lose your $10,000 investment in its entirety. Binary options so closely resemble gambling that they're regulated in exactly the same way by the US Commodity Futures Trading Commission.

There are a number of binary option brokers in the United States of America. The most popular of these are Nadex, RaceOption, Pocket Option, and BinaryCent.

Nadex is by far the most popular option. It was founded by John Nafeh in 2004 and allows its users to take out binary options on everything from stocks that are traded on the major stock exchanges like the NYSE or NASDAQ to the exchange rates of foreign currencies. All you need in order to start taking out binary options on Nadex is $250 to cover the required initial deposit; thereafter the world is your oyster. Each contract that you take out with Nadex will cost you an additional $1, as well as an order fee that can be up to $50.

RaceOption has often been said to be the easiest binary option broker platform to use. Just like Nadex, it allows its users to place binary options on a number of markets from forex to the traditional stock market. It also allows its users to make a number of different binary option trades, namely long-term options, high/low options, one-touch options, 60-second options, and ladder/pair options. Long-term options allow you to hedge a bet on how a stock, currency, or other security will perform over the span of about a week. High/low options ask you to make one simple choice and that is whether a stock, currency, or security will be worth more or less now than when you started taking out the option. One-touch options ask you to predict the exact amount that a stock, currency, or other security will be worth by the end of a predetermined period of time (you need to be exactly correct in order to receive a payout, making it one of the trickier option types). 60-second options let you lock in what you think a stock's price will be and then give you a minute in which to "lock in" (confirm) your binary option. Ladder/pair options allow you to pick a price range that you think a stock, currency, or other currency will fall into at the end of a predetermined period of time. The myriad of binary option types that RaceOption offers means that it suits just about any kind of day trader. Just as is the case with Nadex, you need to deposit at least $250 to open an account and to start trading. Unfortunately RaceOption only allows you to take binary options out of up to 90% of your total investment.

Pocket Option is an international binary option broker with a head office located in the Marshall Islands. What makes Pocket Option truly unique is that it gives its users the opportunity to create a "practice" binary option trading account called a demo-account. This account allows users to execute fake trades with fake money in order to get a feel for binary options trading and allows them to hone their skills before investing any real money in it. You need a lot less money to open an account with Pocket Option than you do to open one with Nadex or RaceOption, as it has a required minimum deposit of only $50 ($200 less than the other two). You can also make more money using Pocket Option because it allows you to receive payouts of up to 128% of the money you put down on a binary option.

BinaryCent is the new kid on the block as it was created late in 2017, but that doesn't mean that its fees are any lower, as it requires the same kind of initial investment as Nadex and RaceOption do: $250. It also allows its users to create demo-accounts and has an incredibly user-friendly mobile application that makes it possible for you to access your account and invest in binary options while having your morning coffee. You can make quite a bit of cash through BinaryCent because they offer awards of up to 90% of the amount that you initially invested on the binary option itself. Like many other binary option brokers, BinaryCent has different account types with different associated costs and benefits: bronze, silver, and gold. You need an initial deposit of $250 to open a bronze account with BinaryCent, but doing so gives you access to a demo-account, to a copy trading tool, and to one-hour withdrawals. A silver account requires an initial deposit of at least $1,000 and gives you access to everything that a bronze account does as well as a web session master class and three risk-free trades. A gold account requires an initial investment of $3,000 and gives its user access to everything that bronze and silver accounts do as well as a personal success manager.

Day trading binary options is as easy as entering into short-term binary options that are set to expire before the day's end. Getting started is as simple as visiting any of the aforementioned binary option brokers' websites or downloading their individual mobile applications and registering an account with them. Binary options are a good choice for day traders who don't have the patience to constantly execute small individual trades in order to make a profit and who would rather hedge their bets on a single transaction.

Commodities and Futures Contracts

You first have to understand what commodities are before you'll be able to understand how you can use them to day trade. Commodities are raw materials, like oil, soy beans, silver, iron, corn, aluminum, gold, and copper, that are used in commerce to produce more finished or refined goods. Of course day traders can't buy piles of corn in the morning and sell them all again by the evening. This means that they're only really able to utilize them in the form of futures contracts.

Futures contracts may sound a bit complicated and scare off some day traders, but they're nothing to be afraid of. In essence a futures contract is a contractual agreement between two companies for the sale and purchase of a commodity at a predetermined price at a later date. An example of a futures contract would be if Johnny agreed to buy 100 of Sarah's apples for $0.05 per apple once they are ripe about a month from now.

Futures contracts can be bought and sold on the Intercontinental Exchange, the New York Board of Trades, and the Chicago Mercantile Exchange, although most brokers and brokerage firms are capable of buying them through their platforms on your behalf.

Day trading commodities in the form of futures contracts is as easy as buying up futures contracts through your broker or one of the aforementioned exchanges and selling them all as their prices increase before the trading day comes to an end. It's important that you check futures contracts' expiration dates before investing in them because if you own them when they expire you're liable for receiving the commodity that is bartered in them—you certainly don't want to end up as the unwilling owner of five tons of potatoes or a shipload of coal.

One of the main problems with day trading commodities is that they aren't very volatile, which means that it's incredibly difficult to exploit any of their price differences for profits.

Forex (Foreign Exchange)

Forex, also called the Foreign Exchange Market and FX, is the name given to the international market of currencies that sees billions of dollars converted to and from euros, pounds, rupees, pesos, rands and other international currencies every single day. These currencies are not evaluated or sold by a central authority; this means that technically all foreign currency exchanges are conducted "over-the-counter."

Why would you want to convert your precious dollars to any other currency? Well, the answer is simple—currencies are volatile, which means that you can increase the amount of dollars you get back out of an exchange by carefully picking currencies that are about to increase in value.

Let's say, for argument's sake, that you purchase $100 worth of South African rands at $17.40 per rand (equaling about R1,740) and you hold onto them until the exchange rate has decreased to $15.00 per rand. If you sold them at this point, you would receive $116 in exchange, this would mean that you made $16 in profit just by waiting for the South African rand to increase in strength against the dollar. Of course, most day traders who are involved in forex trading invest a whole lot more than $100 per exchange.

A country's currency might increase in value for a number of reasons, ranging from the discovery of oil to a favorable election result, and may decrease if its holding country's government racks up too much debt or if there is political instability in the country.

It's important to note that forex trading is considered both a purchase and a sale because when you invest in a foreign currency you are essentially selling your dollars to be able to purchase it.

The easiest way to get involved in forex trading is through your stockbroker or chosen brokerage firm (most of them offer forex services), but if you'd prefer to go solo, you could make use of one of the many online platforms that act as access points to the Foreign Exchange Market. Some of the best forex platforms to make use of are MetaTrader 4, MetaTrader 5, cTrader, and NinjaTrader.

MetaTrader 4 is probably the most basic forex platform that you can make use of, but it is also one of the most popular. It allows its users to invest in all major and many minor forex trading pairs and gives them the option to place market orders, pending orders, and limit orders. This platform also employs an impressive team of expert forex advisors who are always on hand to help you to plan your next move. One of the major downsides of this platform is that it is notably slower than its competitors.

MetaTrader 5 is MetaTrader 4's big brother. It very closely resembles the latter platform but has a number of upgrades, like faster processing times and allowing a wider variety of orders to be placed. For these reasons, it is often more attractive to day traders. Its revolutionary software also allows its users to switch between "netting" (normal) and "hedging" mode. This platform shows its users which trades are complementary to each other when its hedging mode is activated, making it easier for users to insure that they make a profit regardless of which way the market turns.

MetaTrader4 and MetaTrader 5 both have fantastic mobile applications that are available on Windows, iOS, and Android so that you can keep an eye on your forex trades wherever you may be.

cTrader is another very popular platform, but it's different in several ways from both of the previously mentioned ones. It also allows its users to trade a variety of major and minor currency pairs at any time of the day but doesn't offer nearly as much support in the form of chat rooms and advisors as both MetaTrader 4 and MetaTrader 5 do. It also doesn't allow you to use it in conjunction with other trading programs, limiting the amount of customization that can be performed on it.

NinjaTrader is the most expensive of the four platforms I've named because you need to purchase a lifetime, annual, or quarterly subscription to it in order to have access to its forex trading platform. Many argue that it's worth the money, though, because it offers its users automated strategy development, advanced charting, and trade simulation.

Day trading forex is as easy as making forex trades through your broker, brokerage firm, or one of the four forex platforms I've mentioned and making sure that you convert all of your positions back into their original currency before the day's end (if you're an American citizen, then your original currency would have been the dollar). The forex markets never close (unlike most stock exchanges) so the "trading day" takes place between when you wake up and when you go back to bed again.

Chapter 2:

Risk, Cost, Reward

Everything in life is risk and reward: if you go off to college, you're risking losing the money you paid as fees, but the reward should (hopefully) be a degree at the end of a couple of years of study; if you decide to have children, you're risking your financial, physical, and psychological health (especially if you're a woman), but the reward is the love you get to give and receive from your kids; and if you decide to take a higher-paying job, you're taking the risk that you might not like it in exchange for the reward of a bigger paycheck. Just because there's a measure of risk in something doesn't mean that it's not worth doing—this goes for day trading too.

Of course, the rewards that day trading can offer can often entirely blind aspiring day traders to its risks. You should be wary that you do not become blind to risk because, although it is entirely worth it despite the risk involved, it is entirely unwise to ignore it entirely.

How Much Money Can I Expect To Make From Day Trading?

It's difficult to say exactly how much day traders make for two reasons. First, most professional day traders do not like to reveal exactly how much they make per annum and second, the amount they make is largely dependent on the amount that they invest.

The simplest way to quantify how much your average day trader earns is by measuring how much the money they spend day trading grows in a month. A number of studies have done just that and have found that you can expect to make about a 10% return while day trading (with some of the top day traders regularly making returns of more than 20%).

In other words if you spend $1,000 day trading every month, you should make about $100. This might not sound like much, but if you keep reinvesting your profits at the beginning, you'll be making thousands in no time. For example, if you start off by day trading $3,000 today you should have $9415 to trade with by this time next year (assuming that you make a steady 10% return over 12 months and that you reinvest all of your profits). If you keep reinvesting your profits for three years with an initial investment of $3,000, you'll have $92,738 by the end of a 36-month period—that's a lot of money, and it'll mean that within three years you could be pocketing a profit of $9,273.80 every month with a clean $92,738 investment on the backburner in case you ever need it. Of course, your earning potential goes way up if you can make a larger initial investment or if you're willing to keep reinvesting all of your profits for a longer period of time. If you have a natural knack for day trading, you might even be able to achieve returns of 20%. This means that an initial investment of $3,000 over three years would grow to $2,126,405 (as long as you keep reinvesting your profits for the first three years and consistently achieve returns of 20% every month). Once you have $2,126,405 at your disposal, you could earn and pocket up to $425,281 in returns every month (at a rate of 20%) while still having $2,126,405 to reinvest. Imagine what you could do with an extra $425,281 every month.

What Are the Risks Involved in Day Trading?

Earning nearly half a million dollars every month off of an initial investment of $3,000 might sound pretty sweet, but day trading is inherently risky too, and you should always be mindful of this.

There are two risks that you take when you start day trading: the risk of capital loss and the risk of psychological addiction.

You can't really have an honest discussion about day trading without admitting that an awful lot of day traders lose money instead of making it. This doesn't mean that day trading will inevitably lead to you losing money, but it does mean that the majority of traders are doing something very, very wrong.

The first mistake that a lot of new day traders make is giving up too soon. A study that was published by Brad Barber, Yong Lee, Yu-Jane Liu, and Terrance Odean in the *SSRN Electronic Journal* in 2014 found that four-fifths of all new day traders gave up within a single year. If you consider the exponential growth we talked about when we discussed how much money could be made through day trading, it's easy to understand why a day trader might consider themself unsuccessful within the first 12 months of trading. You need to give your portfolio enough time to produce enough profits before you can seriously start day trading, and not having the patience to do so is certainly one of the main reasons that so many day traders fail.

Another study titled *Do Individual Investors Trade Stock as Gambling?* that was published in 2011 found, without the help of charts and analytics, that most day traders were entirely unable to objectively tell their successful trades from their unsuccessful trades. Without this crucial information on hand traders are unable to learn from their mistakes and may continue to trade in ways that essentially cost them money instead of generating it for them. For this reason it's important that you keep track of your trades and whether or not you exited them "in the money" (at a profit), either in the form of a chart or a ledger. If we don't recognize our mistakes, we're entirely unable to learn from them.

Shockingly, the aforementioned study conducted by Barber and his fellow researchers also found that some traders continued day trading for up to a decade despite continuously making losses. This indicates that some day traders not only neglect keeping record of their trades (and thus their trading successes) but that they're also entirely oblivious to whether they're actually making any money or not.

Considering all of the research that's been conducted in this regard, it becomes apparent that a good number of day traders do lose money while day trading, but you shouldn't let this deter you from pursuing your day trading dreams. All that it means is that it's important for you to learn from the mistakes of those who failed.

Luckily many of the pitfalls that trap others are easy to avoid with a good dose of determination and diligence.

The other risk (or rather danger) of day trading is psychological addiction. Day trading feels good, especially if your trades are going your way. It feels so good that some people simply can't stop, even if their trades aren't going their way. The reason for this phenomenon boils down to the similarities between day trading and gambling. People become addicted to both because of psychological or biological predispositions, and this addiction is often reinforced by physical changes that occur in the brains of habitual gamblers. Gambling has the same effect on your brain that drug use has because it encourages your brain to produce up to ten times more dopamine than it usually does. Dopamine is the hormone in your brain that is responsible for making you feel happy and producing feelings of euphoria, and who doesn't enjoy being on cloud nine? The danger is that day trading, just like gambling, can get you hooked on the rush supplied to you by the oversupply of dopamine in your brain. Developing a dependency on this feeling of elation and excitement can lead to you compulsively day trading, even when trades aren't going your way or when you need to use your rent money as capital in order to keep going.

There are a number of ways that you can avoid getting hooked on day trading in an unhealthy way. First, you should designate a certain amount of funds to day trading and avoid pushing any money into it that isn't a part of this originally designated amount. Second, you should set yourself "working hours" (for example, from 9 am to 5 pm) and you should avoid looking at your trades or even thinking about them when it's not during your working hours. And third, you should avoid chasing your losses by reinvesting in trades that are similar to those that you've recently lost money on. If you follow these three simple tips, you should be able to avoid forming any unhealthy habits or addictions.

What Are the Costs Involved in Day Trading?

Okay, here comes the bad news: getting started with day trading is expensive. It's so expensive that your average American can't just start day trading on a whim; they need to save up a little first (and there's absolutely no shame in that). If you want to day trade stocks you need to have (and maintain) at least $25,000 in your trading account at all times. That amount is about five or six months' worth of pay for most people, so this means that saving up this amount just for day trading can be a bit of a challenge.

Luckily there's an app for everything these days. Qapital is a mobile application that you can download on your cellphone or laptop that can do some of the saving for you (although you'll need to connect it to a registered checking account in order to activate it). Qapital rounds up the amount of all of the purchases you make and deposits the difference into your linked checking account. Let's say that you buy a sandwich for $6.20, a coffee for $3.10, and a packet of cigarettes for $5.50 on your way to work every morning. Your Qapital account would round up these amounts to $7, $4, and $6 and deposit $2.20 into your account. If these were the only three things you ever purchased you would manage to save up $554.40 within a year (I seriously doubt that you'd get away with making so few purchases, so this really is a low-ball amount).

Acorns is a money-saving (or rather an investment) app that is rather similar to Qapital. The main difference between it and Qapital is that it invests the money that you save from rounded-up transactions into stocks, exchange traded funds (called ETFs), and mutual funds on your behalf. It even gives you the option to invest passively, a choice that offers lower risks and lower rewards, or to invest aggressively, a choice that has higher associated risks but higher rewards too.

There's a mobile app named Honey that can help you to stash away some cash too. You download it and it then scours the internet looking for coupons and discount codes to apply to any and all of your online purchases. Downloading it can help you to save hundreds of dollars on your purchases, money that you can put away towards that $25,000 initial capital that you need in order to start day trading on the stock market.

The fourth and final mobile app that you should have in your inventory if you're trying to save up in order to start day trading is called Clarity Money. Clarity Money checks what your monthly bills and payments are and tries to negotiate for lower rates and discounts on your behalf wherever possible. It also checks on any subscriptions that you might have and cancels those that it sees that you're not using.

Other than relying on software applications to help you to count your pennies, you can also increase the girth of your savings account by applying some tried and true techniques like carpooling or using public transport to get to work, cooking your own meals at home instead of eating at a restaurant or getting takeout, buying the generic version of products wherever possible (if they're the cheapest option), and cutting down on luxuries like grooming expenses and your cellphone bill.

If saving up $25,000 seems like an insurmountable task, you might consider day trading a commodity with start-up costs that are a little bit lower. It only costs about $1,000 to open a futures contract trading account on most platforms, and that's quite a bit less than $25,000. That might be enough to open an account, but you need about $10,000 to be able to generate enough income from day trading futures contracts in order to be able to do it as a full-time job. The start-up costs associated with day trading commodities are the same as those associated with day trading futures because of the nature of how commodities are traded.

You only need about $500 dollars to start day trading forex because you generally only need an initial deposit of approximately $100 in order to start trading on most platforms (the additional $400 to bring your start-up costs up to $500 is only to insure that you have enough initial capital to start seeing a sufficient level of profits from the moment that you start trading). $500 might be enough to help you start building your investment capital for bigger trades, but it won't generate enough to enable you to trade as a full-time job. If you want to be able to support yourself from day trading forex alone, you should start trading with at least $5,000.

The cheapest commodity to day trade is cryptocurrency. There's generally no required minimum investment in order to start buying and selling cryptocurrencies. This means that you could theoretically start day trading them with as little as $50 in your trading account. Of course, as is the case with all other day trading commodities, the more you invest, the more you'll consequently make. If you want to make a living off of day trading cryptocurrencies from the get-go, you'll need an initial investment of at least $5,000.

Any profits that you make from day trading are also subject to tax. In the United States day traders are exposed to regular income tax rates, unlike the long-term investment tax rates that some long-term stock investors are subject to. If you make less than $9,325 in profit annually from day trading, you'll be subject to income tax of 10%, which means that you'll owe the government $932.50. Income tax rates increase as your profit levels increase. If you make less than $37,950 in profit annually from day trading, you'll be subject to income tax of 15%, which means that you'll owe the government $5692.50 if you earn the entire $37,950. Profits of less than $91,900 are taxed at 25%, profits of less than $191,650 are taxed at 28%, profits of less than $416,700 are taxed at 33%, profits of less than $418,400 are taxed at 35%, and profits of more than $418,400 are taxed at 39.6%.

You might have to give some of the money you make from day trading back to the tax man, but you can also claim some of your losses back from him. As long as you keep all of your trading receipts as proof, you'll be able to claim back up to $3,000 in losses, although you need to wait at least 30 days after making the loss to be able to claim it back. You could claim back even more if you qualify for Trader Tax Status benefits through the Internal Revenue Service (IRS). The qualifying criteria are quite subjective, making it difficult to receive approval under this classification, and include having to almost constantly conduct short-term trades with the goal of exploiting small fluctuations in the market (just like day traders do). If you qualify for Trader Tax Status, you'll be able to claim back a whole bunch of extra expenses like the costs of running your home office, any related educational fees, the depreciation of business assets, the cost of trading software subscriptions, the cost of attending trading seminars, and your start-up expenses. If you're interested in finding out if you qualify for Trader Tax Status you should visit the IRS website.

It's important that you consider all of the costs involved in day trading before getting started to make sure that your new operation remains profitable. It's a good idea to draw up a table of your costs, expenses, and start-up capital to get a better idea of what your initial financial position would be.

Chapter 3:

What You Need To Get

Started

You have most of the theoretical knowledge that you need to get started now, but you're probably still a little bit unsure of how exactly you should go about getting started. Luckily this chapter's sole purpose is to empower you with the practical knowledge that you need in order to make a living from day trading.

You need a couple of things at your disposal if you want to be a successful day trader, the most important of which are a laptop and a reliable internet connection. These basics will allow you to access the trading platforms that enable day trading, which is the bare minimum required for you to start making money. Although any laptop or computer will do in the beginning, you should aim to own a setup with a generous amount of memory and processing power, as trading software often requires a good chunk of both in order to function optimally. If you want to further optimize your setup you might also want to invest in two screens so that you can view analytic charts and your chosen trading platform at the same time. The quality of your internet connection is also rather important. This is because day trading takes place in a matter of minutes, as prices fluctuate up or down by the second. If your internet connection is too slow, it might not be able to load pages fast enough for you to be able to exploit these sudden movements in a timely manner. If you can, you should also try to aim to convert a part of your home into a home office. Creating a quiet space for yourself to work in can help you to concentrate, thus improving the quality of your trading choices and subsequently improving your trading outcomes.

Once you have all of this at your disposal, you can head over to your chosen brokerage firm or trading platform's website and open a demo-account.

Why You Should Start Off With a Demo-Account

As we discussed in chapter two, there are a number of risks associated with day trading, the most prolific of which is financial loss. Most aspiring day traders have never traded on the stock market before, so this means that they're entirely new to reading stock market indicators and choosing profitable stocks. There's absolutely no shame in being a beginner, but do you really want to risk losing actual money while you're still learning the ropes? Of course you don't. I certainly wouldn't. Imagine how horrified you'd be if you managed to save up $25,000 in order to day trade stocks, only to lose most of it on a bad trade because you read a stock chart incorrectly.

Luckily, you can spare yourself the heartache of losing money out of ignorance by opening a demo-account before you ever even consider opening a trading account. A demo-account is quite simply a practice account. It gives you virtual money and an account that resembles a normal trading account with all of the accessories, like stock charts and trading news, that a true trading account would have. It then allows you to use this virtual money to buy and sell simulated stocks that have been programmed to exactly resemble the stocks and their price movements on the real stock market. All of this allows you to conduct trades that feel real and that result in you either making a profit or a loss, giving you an opportunity to hone your skills without having to put real money on the line.

Opening a demo-account will teach you how to make proper use of leverage to increase your profits, it will allow you to test out which trading strategies work best for you, it will give you an opportunity to learn how to navigate your chosen trading platform, and it will help you to form a better understanding of the analytical tools that the platform offers. These are all valuable skills to have before you consider day trading with real money.

There are a number of fantastic day trading simulators out there for you to choose from if you don't opt to go with the one that your chosen trading platform offers.

The most popular ones are MetaTrader 4 demo-accounts, IC Markets demo-accounts, Plus500 demo-accounts, and Etoro demo-accounts.

Getting a MetaTrader 4 demo-account is as simple as downloading MetaTrader 4 and selecting the demo-account option. The MetaTrader 4 software application is compatible with desktops, laptops, tablets, and mobile devices that run Android, Windows, or iOS, so this means that you can access your demo-account from wherever you may be just like a full-time day trader might access their trading account. Another attractive aspect of MetaTrader 4's demo-accounts is the fact that they allow you to practice day trading any asset you could possibly dream of, from stocks to forex. Additionally, most of the account options offered by MetaTrader 4 are completely unlimited, so you can make use of your demo-account for as long as you like. Theoretically you could spend an entire year honing your skills with MetaTrader4's demo-account before moving over to the real thing.

IC Markets' demo-accounts offer more than just a simulated account to practice with, they offer a sense of community. If you're the kind of person that learns best alongside others, it might just be the perfect demo-account for you. This platform is renowned for its active, friendly, and supportive chat rooms and forums, making it easy for its users to tap into the knowledge of others. It has a Windows, iOS, and Android-compatible website and an iOS and Android-compatible mobile application, making it just as accessible as MetaTrader 4's demo-accounts are. It is best known for its sophisticated and high-tech technical analysis tools, like its minute-to-minute stock price charts. IC Markets' demo-accounts, just like MetaTrader 4's demo-accounts, are unlimited, which means that you can practice on them for as long as you would like with absolutely no pressure to spend any real money.

You should only consider Plus500's demo-accounts if you're looking to day trade Contracts for Difference (CFDs). CFDs are contracts that you can invest in and conclude with an investment or brokerage firm. These contracts are based on an underlying asset like a commodity, a stock, or a currency and span the length of an agreed-upon period of time (if you're day trading this period should be less than 24 hours). At the end of this contracted period of time, the investor or brokerage firm that you signed with pays you an amount equal to the difference between the price that the asset was selling for at the beginning of the contracted period and the price it was selling for at the end of the contracted period. If it ends up selling for less at the end of the contracted period than it was selling for at the beginning of the contracted period, you owe the issuing investment or brokerage firm the difference between the two amounts instead. If you think that CFDs may be the thing for you, then you should head over to Plus500's website immediately. Its demo-accounts are unlimited and even resettable; this means that you can scrap all of your trades and start anew at the click of a button, allowing you to continue practicing without the spectres of your past mistakes constantly haunting you. Just like the previous two demo-accounts that we've discussed, Plus500 also has both a wonderfully user-friendly website and a mobile application, which means that you can check on your CFDs while snuggled up on the couch in front of the television.

Etoro's demo-accounts allow you to practice trading the widest variety of assets; it is compatible with forex, cryptocurrencies, stocks, and CFDs. Setting up an Etoro demo-account is as easy as creating an account on their website and clicking on the "practice trading login" button. Etoro is entirely free-to-use, unlimited, and mobile-compatible too and has often been lauded for its user-friendly and simple interface.

You might not be able to start day trading straight away because you may need to save up some start-up capital first, but you could start practicing by setting up a demo-account today. Why waste time doing nothing while you're saving up to make an initial deposit when you could be using that time to familiarize yourself with the art of day trading?

Choosing a Stockbroker

After you've spent some time improving your day trading abilities via a demo-account, it'll be time to start looking for a broker. A stockbroker is a professional person to whom you pay a commission or flat rate fee in exchange for their services in helping you to select trades, negotiating lower trading prices for you, and for executing buy or sell orders on your behalf. Most stockbrokers have a degree in finance, economics, business, or accounting and all of them are required to have passed FINRA's series 63 and series 7 examinations. In years gone by you used to be able to visit your stockbroker at their offices, but these days most of their services have migrated online, so you're likely to interact with your broker only on their online platform or via email.

Simply typing "day trading stockbrokers" into Google will throw up hundreds of thousands of results, but not all stockbrokers were created equally. You should steer clear of brokers and brokerage firms that haven't been personally recommended to you by other traders and day traders, simply because you generally entrust your broker with quite a hefty sum of money and you certainly don't want to engage someone's services when you don't trust them to handle your funds with the utmost diligence and responsibility. If you don't have any trader buddies to recommend a broker to you, allow me to make a few suggestions.

Interactive Brokers is probably the best value you'll get for your money. They're world-renowned for the accurate and user-friendly analytical charts that they make available to their clients, and they're super cheap, only charging about $0.005 per share held on their platform. Paying half a cent per share for expert advice and guidance sounds like a pretty good deal to me. Interactive Brokers might be cheap, but they'll penalize you for being the same. Unfortunately you are likely to incur charges known as inactivity fees if your account with this online brokerage firm falls below $100,000, an amount that few day traders will have at their disposal when they're just starting off. One of Interactive Broker's most attractive features is the fact that it allows its clients to make automated trades by pre-selecting set, programmed trading strategies and applying them to their chosen financial security like stocks, forex, or cryptocurrencies.

If you're looking for as much guidance as possible while still having access to things like trade histories, stock projections, and various market indicators, TradeStation might be your best bet. This online brokerage firm offers two tiered platforms, TradeStation Go and TradeStation Select. TradeStation Go is the cheaper option because it doesn't have a required initial deposit, charges no fees on stock and ETF trades, and only charges $0.50 on every options contract that you take out. TradeStation Select is the premium option and consequently it requires an initial deposit of $2,000, although trades made on stocks and ETFs are free just as they are with TradeStation Go. It's also a bit more expensive to trade options with TradeStation Select because it charges $0.60 per option traded. Its most attractive feature is similar to that of Interactive Broker in that it allows you to make automated trades, but the difference is that it allows you to program in triggers that you would like it to trade off of.

TD Ameritrade is an online brokerage firm that rivals Interactive Brokers when it comes to affordability, except unlike Interactive Brokers it doesn't require that you keep a minimum amount of $100,000 in your trading account at all times in order to avoid incurring additional charges. It has no required initial minimum investment, its brokers don't charge any commission fees, and it'll even give you a startup bonus of $600 once you've funded your account (who doesn't need an extra $600 as start-up capital?). It also has an interactive trading platform called thinkorswim that allows you to keep track of trading charts and other analytic tools in real-time while also viewing your dashboard and portfolio. To round it all off, it also has a fantastic mobile application that is compatible with Android and iOS, allowing you to make trades and keep an eye on the market from anywhere in the world, so that someday you could be sitting on your own private yacht drifting around a Caribbean island while checking up on your TD Ameritrade trades from your iPhone.

If you're looking to engage the services of the online brokerage firm that is best known for its incredibly fast execution times, you should look no further than Lightspeed. It has some of the best customer service and advisor ratings, but it is unfortunately a bit more expensive than the aforementioned three online brokerage firms. It charges about $0.0045 per share if you own less than 249,999 shares, $4.50 per trade if you conduct less than 250 trades per month, $0.60 per options contract if you own less than 500 contracts, and $1.29 per futures contract. Their fees get lower and lower as you conduct more trades and invest in more financial securities. A lot of traders believe that it's worth the extra expense because it's also arguably the most private and secure online brokerage firm around, thanks largely to the virtual private network (VPN) that it is run through. The most prolific downside to Lightspeed is the fact that you can't trade forex through any of their platforms.

If you're an absolute beginner and would thus like to spend as little money as possible while receiving as much guidance as possible, then Tastyworks is the online brokerage firm for you. It is incredibly cheap, has no required minimum initial deposit, and doesn't charge commission or additional fees on trades involving stocks (although you should expect to pay about a dollar for every options contract that you enter into). It is best known for the educational materials that it offers its clients, not only giving them analytical tools to use but teaching them how to use them. Of course, it also has some downsides. For example, it only allows its clients to invest in financial securities from the United States and it doesn't offer them a demo-account with which to practice before diving into the real thing.

Whichever stockbroker or brokerage firm you decide to go with, it's important that you consider the associated fees, ease of transactions and trades, withdrawal and deposit time frames, and execution time frames before making your choice.

Chapter 4:

Becoming Knowledgeable

Hopefully by now you've already opened your browser to create a demo-account on one of the previously suggested platforms. But you've still got a bit of learning to do before you'll really be able to call yourself a day trader.

Education and learning are ongoing processes. If you really want to be the best day trader that you could possibly be, and if you're serious about maximizing your profits, then you should set aside an hour or two every day and use it to increase your knowledge of the stock market, commodities, currencies, and cryptocurrencies by reading books (like this one), watching instructional videos and vlogs, and perusing financial news websites.

If you make perpetual learning your goal, then you'll see perpetual improvements in your profit margins.

Important Day Trading Terms and Their Definitions

If you're going to be the next George Soros, then you're going to have to learn the lingo. Lawyers speak in legalese and doctors are fluent in medical nomenclature, so you should be comfortable with stock trading jargon. Being able to "speak the language" isn't just important because it allows you to understand what stockbrokers and your fellow traders are saying, it's important because it'll help them to take you seriously as a roleplayer in the stock market. Penetrating the upper echelons of the stock trading society is an important part of making your way to becoming one of the best day traders to have ever lived.

Following is an extensive list of words and terms relating to stock trading that you should commit to memory and memorize by heart. Working a few of these into your next conversation with your stockbroker or stock trading buddies is a good way to let them know that you're serious about day trading and that you're learning all that you can about it. And you might even be able to use them to confuse or frazzle those who have not been initiated into the world of day trading yet.

Active management: When an account is actively managed, it means that someone (whether this is you, a broker, or a fund manager) is constantly watching your portfolio, making decisions on individual stocks based on their observed performance and noted trends. The stocks in actively managed accounts are also usually hand-picked, meaning that they're chosen on their own merit instead of on whether or not they appear on any of the major stock indices.

Aftermarket: You buy a share on the aftermarket (also called the secondary market) when you buy it from a fellow stock trader instead of the company that originally issued it.

Agency security: When shares, bills, or notes originate from a federal agency, they are known as agency securities.

American depository receipts: If you purchase stocks in a foreign company on an American stock exchange, you are actually purchasing American depository receipts (ADRs). ADRs are issued by the government and are the equivalent of owning a real share in the company that they belong to.

American Stock Exchange (AMEX): The previous name of the New York Stock Exchange (NYSE American). It was acquired (and its name was consequently changed) by the NYSE in 2008.

Annual report: The United States' Securities and Exchange Commission (SEC) requires by law that all publicly traded companies publish an annual report on a yearly basis. This report must contain information on the company's financial details, its fiduciary performance, its market segment, the result of its operations, its subsidiary activities, and new product plans.

Arbitrage: This is a day trading strategy that involves buying stock on one stock exchange only to sell it for a tiny profit on another, thus exploiting the price differences on the different trading platforms. In modern times arbitrage is a bit more difficult to pull off because stock prices are updated in real time, meaning that any price differences between platforms are usually miniscule and momentary.

Ask: The price of purchase of an individual stock.

At-the-money: A stock is said to be at-the-money when it reaches the price at which you're looking to buy or sell it.

Auction market: This is a stock exchange in which the price is a midpoint between the least amount of money the seller is willing to accept for a certain stock and the most amount of money that a buyer is willing to pay for it. An example of a market that follows this format is the NYSE.

Average: See *stock market index*.

Away from the market: These are orders that tell the manager of a portfolio (whether that's you or a broker) to buy stocks or sell stocks at a price that is currently unattainable. This order can only be executed once the price of a stock rises or falls to meet the point set by the portfolio-holder. This means that in day trading this order should only be given when you're relatively certain that your set price point will be achieved during the trading day.

Banker's acceptance: These are essentially an "I owe you" from the bank. They come into existence when the bank "loans" money from an individual or institution and they represent a promise to repay this amount with interest. Banker's acceptances are traded at fluctuating prices between traders on the aftermarket much like stocks belonging to publicly-traded companies are.

Basis: This is the total amount of money that you pay to buy stock belonging to a certain company, including any commissions or fees that are payable along with its initial purchase price.

Bear: No, this isn't an adorable woodland creature. This is someone who believes that the stock market is about to experience a down swing, meaning that stock prices will decrease across the board. Bears are more likely to sell on impulse than they are to buy on impulse.

Bear market: A bear market occurs when the stock market really is experiencing a down swing that is leading to a decline in stock prices. In long-term stock trading a bear market is the idle time to buy stocks, although it doesn't really affect day trading's timing.

Bear raid: No, this isn't an organized attack by a guerilla group of adorable woodland creatures. A bear raid is however relevant to day trading. It occurs when traders purposefully undersell a certain stock (sell it for less than its inherent market value) in order to decrease its value on the stock exchange. This is usually done to make hoarding a massive amount of these stocks in one large purchase possible.

Bearer securities: These are securities that are loosely traded because their issuing companies don't keep track of who owns them. The fact that their issuing company doesn't know who owns them can make claiming dividends a little tricky, although this is more relevant to stock trading in general and will be less of a concern to a day trader.

Beta: This is a number value assigned to a stock that represents how volatile its price is when compared to stocks that are held in Standard and Poor's 500 Index (S&P 500 Index). The higher a stock's beta value is, the more prone its price is to fluctuating. A stock that has a beta of 3.0 will decrease 30% in price where a stock on the S&P 500 Index would only fall by 10% while a stock with a beta value of 0.5 will only decrease in value by 5% where a stock on the S&P 500 Index would fall by 10%.

Bid: This is the most amount of money that traders are willing to pay for stock in a specific company.

Block: This is a term used to refer to a trade that involves a very large number of stocks (usually more than 10,000 shares belonging to the same company).

Blow-Off Top: This is an effect that is best observed on a chart representing the rise and fall of a certain stock's price. It is characterized by a sharp upward movement as the stock's price drastically increases, followed by a sharp decline in the movement of the stock's price as it suddenly decreases. It is mostly used in technical analysis when you're trying to decide whether to incorporate a certain stock into your portfolio.

Blue-chip stocks: These are stocks that belong to large, national companies that regularly produce impressive profits and that are well-traded and well-respected on the stock exchanges that they trade on. They're often included in stock market and benchmark indices.

Breadth of market: This is a value, normally expressed as a ratio, that is used in security analysis. Its main purpose is to show whether the emerging market is a bear market or a bull market. It is usually expressed as the number of shares that have increased in value over a given period of time in relation to the number of shares that have decreased in value over a given period of time.

Breakout: This is something that those who trade using technical analysis keep an eye out for. It is when a stock's price increases to above its previous record high (or 52-week high) or when its price decreases to below its previous record low (or 52-week low). When a breakout occurs in either direction, it shows technical analysts that that specific stock's price is likely to continue following that trend.

Bull: A bull is essentially the opposite of a bear. It is an investor who firmly believes that the stock market is going to experience an upswing soon and that stock prices will consequently increase across the board. Bulls are more prone to impulse buying than they are to impulse selling.

Bull market: This is when the stock market really does experience an upswing that leads to a general increase in the asking price of stocks. In long-term stock trading it is the ideal time to sell shares, although it doesn't really affect day trading strategies.

Buying power: This is a term that is used to refer to the amount of liquid capital that a trader has with which they can purchase stocks and securities. In a margin account it also includes any capital that is on loan to the trader.

Call: This is a type of option that gives a trader the choice to buy stocks at a pre-agreed price when they reach a certain price point. You might have a "call" with your broker if you have asked them to buy 100 shares in Apple when (and if) its stock price reaches $280. However, having this option in place does not obligate the trader to execute the trade when the pre-agreed price point is reached (that's why it's called an option!).

Capital gain: This is the amount that a stock's price increases between its point of purchase and its point of sale. For example, if you buy one share in Apple for $320 and then sell it again for $322, your capital gain will be two dollars.

Certificate: This is a piece of paper that you're issued when you purchase most kinds of stocks. It can be used to prove ownership and facilitate further trade. Certificates aren't issued for bearer securities.

Chicago Board Options Exchange (CBOE): This is an options exchange that is (you guessed it) located in Chicago. It is the largest of its kind in the entire United States of America and hosts more than 2,300 companies that trade nearly 1.3 billion contracts (options) every year.

Close: This can be used to refer to two things, namely the time at which a specific stock exchange closes for the day and the price that a certain stock was trading at when the stock exchange it is trading on closed for the day. Most of the major American stock exchanges (like the NYSE and NASDAQ) close at 4pm every day.

Commission: This is a fee that is normally charged by brokers on every sale of stocks that you make. It is usually calculated as a percentage of the total income into your trading account.

Common stock: If you own stocks in America, they belong to one of two classes; they're either classified as common stock or they're classified as preferential stock. Common stock is normally traded publicly and allows its owner to vote on matters relating to its holding company, to have a say in the election of the board of directors, and to benefit from any dividend payouts that its holding company may issue. In Britain (and in countries that used to be British colonies) they're referred to as ordinary shares.

Convertible preferred stock: Common stocks are so cool that you might want to trade your preferred stocks in for a couple of them. Luckily there's a type of preferred stock that allows you to do just that. This kind of stock can be put over into common stock for a price at a later date.

Corner a/the market: If you're cornering a/the market it means that you've bought such a substantial amount of stocks belonging to a single company that you're technically capable of forcing its stock prices to increase or decrease depending on the "ask" that you put on the stocks that you do control.

Cyclicals: These are stocks whose prices regularly fluctuate in predictable ways because of external factors influencing the market segment that they operate in. Ice cream and swimwear manufacturers are examples of cyclical companies because their profits increase during the summer months when the weather is good enough for a trip to the beach and they decrease in winter when their normal customers are huddled up in front of a heater at home. If you can identify the stocks that are cyclical (and if you can understand what the factors are that induce their cyclical nature), then you're capable of making more informed predictions on whether a stock's price is going to increase or decrease in the near future.

Day order: This is an order that you can give to a stockbroker instructing them to buy or sell a specific share if its price rises or falls to a certain point during the trading day on which the day order is effective. This order is only effective on the trading day that it is given for. It and the instruction that it embodies ceases to exist when the stock market closes for the day.

Debit balance: This is the amount of money that a brokerage firm lends you to supplement your margin account.

Defensive stocks: These kinds of stocks' prices generally remain unwavering and largely unchanged regardless of any external or internal forces that drive other stocks' prices down. They are usually a good investment option for long-term stock investors, but the fact that their prices are unlikely to change on any given day generally makes them a terrible investment for day traders.

Derivative: This is a stock whose price is largely determined by the value of an underlying asset. An example of a derivative stock would be Exxon Mobil or Chevron, whose stock price often depends on the performance of the price of oil.

Discount: This is when a certain stock sells for even less than it sold for when it was originally issued by its holding company.

Divergence: This is when one of the major stock market indices is bullish while another is bearish. When it occurs, it can be difficult for traders to predict whether the stock market is going to experience an overall upswing or an overall downswing, affecting their ability to strategize as well as they might otherwise have been able to.

Dow Jones Industrial Average (DJIA): This is a stock market index that tracks 30 of the United States of America's largest and most successful companies. Some of the companies that it tracks are Disney, Goldman Sachs, Boeing, Chevron, Coca-Cola, Microsoft, McDonald's, Walmart, Verizon, and Visa.

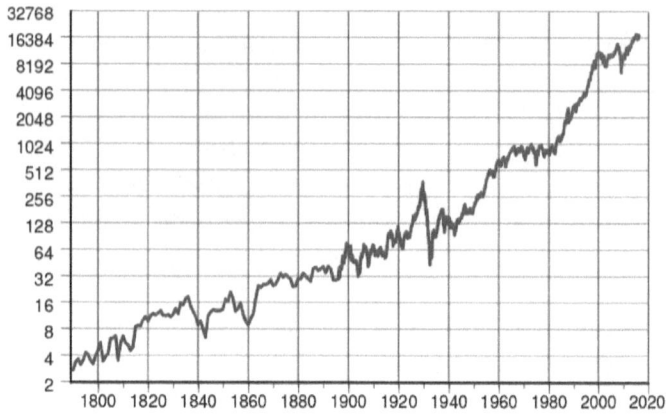

Dow Jones Industrial Average

Electronic communication network (ECN): This is a platform (usually an online platform) on which traders can buy and sell stocks from and to other traders while largely remaining anonymous. It is not a traditional stock exchange but facilitates trade none the less. It is generally the cheaper option for executing large trades, and many traders are naturally drawn to it because they can remain enigmas while day trading.

Endorsement: In order to be able to trade a stock certificate, it needs to be made negotiable. This is normally done by signing its flip side to prove that the person in possession of it is also the person that is listed as its owner on its front side.

Equity options: Taking out an equity option gives you the right to buy a set amount of shares for a pre-agreed sum on or before a predetermined date or time. When you take out an equity option, it usually grants you the right to buy 100 shares for a predetermined price. Traders make use of equity options to lock sellers into a lower price point on the sale of shares just before their prices are expected to increase again. Of course this means that you need to be able to successfully predict market trends in order to make use of them to turn a profit.

European-style option: This is a type of option that gives you the right to buy or sell shares from or to a specific seller for a predetermined price. What makes European-style options different is that you can only "execute" them (make the trade you were planning to make) on the day that the option is set to expire.

Ex-dividend date: This term refers to the day on which a stock's price is decreased because its stockholders have just received dividend payouts. Dividend payouts decrease a stock's price because once they're made, it's likely to be quite a while before they're made again, meaning that they're a less profitable option for prospective buyers.

Execution: When stocks are effectively bought or sold, traders say that they've been "executed." A trade is fully executed when the prospective buyer pays the purchase sum of the stocks that they're looking to acquire.

Expiration date: This is the final day that you can exercise an option on.

Fast market: A fast market occurs when an unexpectedly large amount of stocks are bought within a small time frame. It can lead to trading delays, but it can also lead to a drastic increase in stock prices across the board.

Fill or kill (FOK) order: A FOK order is an order that you give your broker in which you tell them to buy or sell a certain amount of stocks belonging to a specific company for a set price within a predetermined period of time. An example of this would be if you told your broker to buy 100 shares in Apple for $320 per share before the stock market's close today. If Apple's shares traded for $322 for the entire day, it would mean that your broker wouldn't be able to execute your order and it would thus be "killed" (become null and void).

Financial Industry Regulatory Authority (FINRA): This is a non-profit association that is overseen by the SEC whose main purpose in the stock market is to regulate the way that over-the-counter stock brokerage firms operate.

Fractional shares: Sometimes under special circumstances (like in stock splits) you can buy "pieces" of a single share, called a fractional share. Unfortunately they're only made available under exceptional circumstances and you won't be able to buy them on a traditional stock exchange like the NYSE or NASDAQ.

Financial Times Stock Exchange (FTSE) 100 Index: This is a stock market index that tracks 100 of the largest and most successful publicly traded companies that are listed on the London Stock Exchange (LSE). Some of the companies that it tracks are Aveva, Barclays, Autotrader, British American Tobacco (BAT), Prudential, Pearson, Unilever, Vodafone, and Tesco.

Futures contract: A future is a bit like an option, except instead of giving you the right to buy a certain number of stocks for a predetermined price within a set period of time, it locks you into the purchase of a certain number of stocks for a predetermined price at a future date. Unlike an option, you can't back out of a futures contract.

Good till canceled order: This is an order that you give your broker instructing them to buy or sell a set number of stocks for a specified price. Unlike a FOK order, this order stands indefinitely. This means that if you give your broker a good till canceled order instructing them to buy 100 shares in Apple for $290 today, then your broker will wait for 100 stocks in Apple to reach this price point (however long it may take) before executing the sale, unless of course you were to cancel the instructing order before then.

Hedge/hedging: You're hedging if you buy stocks in Exxon Mobil (an oil company) and in Siemens (a renewable energy company) in order to insure that you profit regardless of the market sentiment. If oil prices drop because of environmental concerns, then your Siemens stocks will increase in value, and if the oil industry is doing very well while the renewable energy sector is experiencing its growing pains, then your

Exxon Mobil stocks will increase in value—either way, you win.

House requirement: The least amount of money that you need to have in your trading account in order for it to remain open at a specific brokerage firm.

Immediate or cancel (IOC) order: This is a type of order that you can give to your broker instructing them to immediately buy or sell a set number of stocks for a specific amount of money. If your broker cannot immediately fulfill this order, then it is canceled. An example of an IOC order would be if you told your broker to buy 100 shares in Apple for $280 per share. If the current price of Apple shares was $290 per share, then the order would be canceled, but if the current price of Apple shares was $270 per share, then it would have been executed.

Initial public offering (IPO): This is when a new publicly traded company issues shares that are available to the general public for the very first time. These stocks are known as IPO stocks.

Insider information: This is information that is usually only held by directors and employees of a holding company (or their relatives). It is essentially information that, when it is eventually made public, will drastically influence the stock's base price. It normally involves the resignation or hiring of directors or data on the company's financial performance during the current fiscal year. Employees and directors that are privy to this information often share it with shareholders in order to make a quick buck, but beware—making trades using this knowledge is illegal and is known as "insider trading."

Large-cap stocks: Companies are called "large-cap" companies when their inherent value is more than $5 billion. Large-cap stocks are stocks that are issued by these companies.

Last: This is a term that is used to refer to the most recent price that a certain stock has sold for. For example, if the most recent sale of Apple stocks saw one share trading for $318, then its "last" is said to be $318.

Limit order: This is an order that you give to your stockbroker instructing them to not sell specific stocks for less than a certain amount or not to buy certain stocks for more than a certain amount. For example, you could give your broker a limit order instructing them not to buy Apple stocks for more than $320 per stock. If given this order, your broker will continue to acquire Apple stocks on your behalf unless their price rises to exceed $320 per share.

Limited trading authorization: This is when you give someone else access to your trading account, allowing them to execute trades and to make changes to your portfolio on your behalf. It is usually given to brokers in order to allow them to fully manage your account.

Liquidity: This term refers to how easily you'll be able to sell a stock once you've acquired it. Sought-after stocks, like Apple and Microsoft, are said to be highly liquid because you'll never struggle to find a buyer for them.

Liquidity ratio: This is a number, expressed as a ratio, that is used to reflect how vulnerable a stock's price is to change because of its trading volume. It is calculated by working out how many dollars would need to be spent on a specific stock in order to drive down or to increase its base price on the stock market. Day traders can use this ratio to try and determine whether a stock's price is about to experience a short-term increase or decrease.

Margin: You're said to be buying on margin when you're using money that you've borrowed from your stockbroker or a brokerage firm in order to buy stocks. Of course, this money is only a loan and needs to be paid back to your stockbroker or brokerage firm eventually. You shouldn't buy on margin unless you're absolutely sure that you're going to make enough money off of the trade it is financing in order to pay it back.

Mark-to-market: This is when you keep an eye on a certain stock's price performance over a period of days and weeks so that you are more empowered to decide whether purchasing it is the right move for your day trading strategy.

Market capitalization: This is a number value that is used to reflect the size and the success of a specific company on the stock market. It is calculated by multiplying the amount of shares that the company has issued by their value. The measure of market capitalization gave rise to the concept of large-cap and small-cap stocks.

Market order: This is an order that you give to your broker instructing them to buy or sell a specific amount of stocks as soon as possible for the best price possible. Giving this kind of order means that your broker will have to use their personal discretion to decide when the best time to buy or sell is.

Minus tick: A minus tick occurs when you're able to buy a stock for a lower price than it sold for during its previous "last." It can be an indication that you've made a good trade, but it can also indicate that a stock is experiencing a period of decline (meaning that your investment is in danger of experiencing a further decline in value too).

NASDAQ: NASDAQ used to stand for the National Association of Securities Dealers Automated Quotations System at its inception in 1971, but it has since risen to transcend this abbreviation entirely. It is well-known by stock traders all around the world because fifty years ago it was the very first stock exchange to ever operate electronically. It is the second largest stock exchange in the United States of America (behind the NYSE) and trades in more than $10 trillion worth of stocks and securities from more than 3,500 different companies. Its trading floor is located in New York.

New issue: This is when a publicly traded company issues new shares to be traded on the stock market. These shares can either be issued as a part of an IPO or they can be additional shares that the company has issued in order to raise capital.

New York Stock Exchange (NYSE): The NYSE is one of the oldest stock exchanges in the world (having been founded more than 200 years ago) and it is definitely the world's largest stock exchange, hosting stocks from more than 2,500 different companies equating to more than $23 trillion in market capitalization. Just like the NASDAQ (and as its name suggests) it is located in New York. Four-fifths of the companies that have been included in the S&P 500 Index are also featured on the NYSE.

Noise: This is a term that is used to refer to occurrences in the stock market that are not significant indicators of its future movements and that can confuse analytic traders if they do not recognize them for what they are and ignore them in their considerations. An example of "noise" would be an increase in a stock's price because of a large one-off purchase of it made by a rich investor. This short-term price increase would not be indicative of the fact that the stock is set to continue experiencing sustained growth.

Open: "Open" refers to when a stock exchange starts operating at the beginning of a trading day. Most of the major stock exchanges in the United States of America (like the NYSE and NASDAQ) open at 9:30am.

Over-the-counter (OTC) market: These are platforms that stocks are traded on, but they are not official stock exchanges. In the past they used to be made up of an intricate web of telephonic communications but presently most of them are hosted online. OTC markets are generally the only place that you'll be able to buy publicly traded pink sheet stocks although you may struggle to get your hands on blue chip stocks through them.

Penny stocks: Penny stocks are also often referred to as pink sheets. They're stocks that sell for much less than normal stocks do, usually being traded for less than $5 a pop. You can't buy penny stocks on most conventional stock exchanges, which means that you might have to resort to using an OTC market if you'd like to get your hands on some.

Put: A put is essentially the opposite of an option. A put entitles its holder to sell a predetermined number of stocks for a set price to whoever issued the put. Day traders can use puts to insure that they sell their stocks for higher prices even when the market has driven their inherent value down.

Quote: Most stock exchanges make real-time quotes on all of their stocks available to interested parties and prospective buyers. These quotes show the highest bid on a certain stock as well as its lowest offer at any given time. Quotes were not always up to date before the digitalization of the stock market, but luckily this is no longer an obstacle that traders have to concern themselves with.

Range: This is a term that is used to refer to the difference between the highest amount that a stock has sold for and the lowest amount that it has sold for over the period of time that is being considered. A stock's range can be used to determine its general volatility, meaning it's a useful bit of information for day traders.

Resistance: All stocks have a resistance level (also referred to as a resistance point). This is the point at which their price just doesn't seem to be able to increase anymore. You can extrapolate a stock's resistance level by plotting its prices out on a chart over an extended period of time. Day traders can use this information to determine whether a stock's price is about to move up or down.

Russell 2000 Index: This is a stock market index that tracks stocks belonging to 2,000 smaller companies. It was founded about 40 years ago by the Frank Russell

Company. The stocks that it features are also sold on the NYSE and NASDAQ.

Small-cap stocks: This is a term that is used to refer to smaller companies whose overall market capitalization is less than $1 billion.

Stock market index: An index is made out of a number of companies that represent a cross-section of a particular sector of the market and thus it can be used to approximate the average value and performance of companies belonging to this sector. It is also called an "average" because it represents the average company belonging to a certain market segment.

Stop order: This is an order that you can give to your stockbroker instructing them to buy or sell a certain stock when its price enters a predetermined range. Placing this kind of order can help you to stay ahead of any trends that you may have predicted in the stock market while helping you to step away from your computer screen for a while.

Stop-loss order: This is an order that you can give to your stockbroker instructing them to sell a certain stock if its price falls below a predetermined point. Traders give their brokers this order to make sure that they don't wait too long to offload a stock.

Symbol: A stock's symbol, also called its ticker, is the abbreviation that it is known by on the stock market. For example, Apple's symbol is AAPL, Tesla's symbol is TSLA, Microsoft's symbol is MSFT, and Disney's symbol is DIS.

Technical analysis: Most day traders make trading choices based on technical analysis. Technical analysis is when you compile data that is based on a stock's price movements over a certain period of time and try to extrapolate its future trajectory from this. Technical analysts make use of all kinds of tools from candlestick charts to momentum indicators. In essence technical analysis reveals the market psychology behind a stock's price movements.

You Don't Need a University Degree To Become Knowledgeable

A lot of people are put off of day trading because they labor under the erroneous idea that you need to have a degree in finance or economics in order to be able to do it successfully, but this is simply not true. However, there is a measure of truth to the idea that you need to be educated in order to do it successfully. Luckily, colleges and universities aren't the only ways to become educated. You can educate yourself.

I personally believe that the easiest way to learn about day trading (other than reading this book) is by attending a couple of courses offered by day traders who have been successful themselves. Fortunately in this day and age you don't need to drive hundreds of miles to attend boring seminars because you could simply take part in one of the many online day trading courses offered by well-known and verified traders.

I personally suggest taking part in one hosted by Warrior Trading, Bear Bull Traders, Investor's Business Daily, Market Rebellion, Udemy, Bulls on Wall Street, Better System Trader, or Investors Underground.

Warrior Trading offers two different types of day trading courses, one to fit each kind of pocket. They're called Warrior Starter and Warrior Pro. Warrior Starter is the lowest-tier trading course that they offer, but that doesn't mean that it is second-rate. It consists of fifteen chapters that covers topics like market psychology, technical analysis, fundamental analysis, and account types. Once you've completed these chapters, you then gain access to a demo-account to practice your newly acquired knowledge on as well as access to the group's live chat room where you can ask for advice and keep an eye out for market tips. It costs about $997 to enroll, a reasonable price when you consider that some of their reviewers claim to be earning $1,500 per day trading stocks after completing the course.

Warrior Pro is Warrior Trading's premium trading course. It covers all of the course material covered in the Warrior Starter course and it also covers specialist trading strategies like swing trading, day trading, cryptocurrencies, small-cap stocks, large-cap stocks, and options contracts. Just as is the case with their Warrior Starter course, enrolling in it will give you instant access to a demo-account (that they refer to as a simulated trading account) as well as the group's live chat room. Additionally, it gives you the benefit of six group mentoring sessions every week and access to all of the group's scanner settings. You can enroll in Warrior Trading's Warrior Pro course for as little as $4,297 for 9o days or $5,997 per year.

Bear Bull Traders is a fantastic learning platform for beginner day traders, and it might just be the perfect fit for you if you're looking for a really interactive educational course. There are three possible subscription options: Monthly, Lifetime: 12 Installments, and Lifetime: One Payment. Their Monthly subscription option only costs $99 per month and gives you access to their live chat room between 9am and 4pm Eastern Standard Time (EST), day trading and general stock trading lessons, the group's scanner settings, the group's options trading fundamentals, and a simulated trading account.

Bear Bull Traders' Lifetime: 12 Installments and Lifetime: One Payment options cost about $199 per month and $1,999 respectively. Both of these options give you access to everything that their monthly subscription option gives you access to. You also get access to weekly webinars that cover a variety of trading topics and the group's psychology resources.

Investor's Business Daily has been paving the way for beginner stock and day traders for more than 30 years so they're somewhat of an authority on the subject. They currently offer three different courses that may be valuable to the uninitiated in day trading, namely The Basics of Options Trading, Options Trading Strategies, and Spread Trading. Their Basics of Options course costs about $299 and consists of eight video lessons that cover topics like the science of calls and puts, selecting strike prices, and calculating premiums.

Their Options Trading Strategies course costs a bit more at $399. It consists of nine video lessons that cover topics like selecting a strategy, using risk graphs, using puts to get discounts, taking options out against your own stocks, and using options to insure your portfolio.

It costs $399 to enroll in their Spread Trading course too. Enrolling in it gives you access to 10 educational videos that cover topics like the types of spreads that you can invest in, non-directional positions, and multi-legged positions.

To sweeten the deal, Investor's Business Daily allows you to enroll in all three courses for just $897 (that's a $200 discount) if you enroll in all three at the same time.

Udemy is an online educational platform that was founded in 2009. It hosts lecturers and their courses pertaining to everything from horse care to quantum physics. It has about 57,000 different lecturers (also called instructors) on its platform and approximately 50 million students. Luckily this wonderful internet resource also boasts a number of commendable day trading courses, the best of which are The Complete

Day Trading Course, Four Strategies That Will Make You A Professional Day Trader, and Day Trading 101: How to Day Trade Stocks for Passive Income. As an added bonus, Udemy courses tend to be quite a lot more affordable than many of your other options.

The Complete Day Trading Course costs about $15 to enroll in and has been embarked upon by more than 4,000 very satisfied students. It consists of nearly eight hours' worth of instructional videos and multiple articles and educational resources. It covers topics like trading strategies, charting tools, chart time frames, short selling, the different types of day trading orders, and paper trading. Upon completing it you also get a lovely certificate of completion to frame and hang on your wall.

The Four Strategies That Will Make You A Professional Day Trader course only costs about $12 to enroll in, making it even more affordable than The Complete Day Trading Course. It has been attended by nearly 2,000 students who have reviewed it well over the years. It consists of five hours of educational videos and two practice tests, and covers topics like picking stocks to day trade, making use of the four different gap types to facilitate day trading, when to exit a trade, when to enter a trade, making use of moving averages, and choosing a stockbroker for day trading. Just as is the case with The Complete Day Trading Course, you'll get a certificate of completion to prove that you have successfully completed the course once you pass the final test.

Day Trading 101: How To Day Trade Stocks for Passive Income is currently retailing at $120, making it one of the most expensive Udemy options. It has been attended by more than 3,000 students and is run by Luca Moschini of Sharper Trades. It consists of nearly four hours of instructional videos and three educational articles. It covers topics like reading technical charts, identifying areas of resistance and support, recognizing spikes and drops in stock prices, price breakouts, analyzing a stock's price and volume activity, and spotting moving stocks. It also includes a certificate of completion at its end.

Market Rebellion is a traders' group that was created by Jon Najarian (a former linebacker for the Chicago Bears and currently a very successful day trader). It has a wonderful education platform that offers day trading mentorship opportunities as well as specialized courses focusing on options and cryptocurrency trading. You need to be a member of this group in order to view their educational resources fully, and membership generally comes at a premium. If you'd like access to their webinars, you should consider opening a TNT Options or Time Bandit account at a price of approximately $495 per annum. That might seem like a lot of money, but it's actually a bargain when you consider that Market Rebellion charges about $300 per hour of one-on-one coaching.

Bulls on Wall Street offers its clients access to a 60-day Trading Bootcamp. This course is taught by a successful day trader named Kunal Desai, who also happens to be the chief-executive-officer (CEO) of the company. He has also notably been mentioned by major publications like Forbes, the Huffington Post, Inc.com, and Fortune. Bulls on Wall Street's Trading Bootcamp includes lessons on swing trading, day trading, trading plans, trade recaps, and trading scans. Enrolling in it also gives you a chance to have a one-on-one video chat with Kunal Desai himself in order to discuss your portfolio and trading strategy, interactive quizzes, and two months' access to the group's day trading chat room. It costs about $2,850 to enroll in this course.

Better System Trader also offers seven day trading courses called System Trading Unleashed, Fourteen Day Breakout Strategy Challenge, Build Emini Breakout Strategies Fast, The Breakout Strategies Masterclass, Building Robust Trading Strategies Masterclass, Trading Market Internals, and Smashing False Breakouts. System Trading Unleashed is taught by a systemic market analyst and stockbroker named Martin Lembak. Lembak has been trading stocks for more than 15 years and believes he has personally executed over 1,000 trades during this time period. Lembak's course consists of six modules that cover topics like the best markets to invest in, the best time frames to trade with, choosing an effective trading strategy, popular trading software, recommendations on computer setups for day trading, re-optimizing old trading strategies, the recommended length of execution of various trading strategies, the amount of money you can expect to make when using specific day trading strategies, the most commonly made mistakes, and building your portfolio to maximize your profits. While the course itself is undoubtedly invaluable, it isn't too expensive and you should expect to be able to enroll in it for about $197.

Better System Trader's Fourteen Day Breakout Strategy Challenge course takes only about two weeks to complete and you only need to commit to spending about half an hour on it per day in order to finish it in time. It is taught by an authority on stock trading breakouts, Tomas Nesnidal. Nesnidal has managed a profitable hedge fund for more than three years. This course will equip you with a number of invaluable skills that will enable you to use Nesnidal's signature "combination screening" techniques to spot profitable stocks and futures. Nesnidal claims that you should start seeing a marked improvement in your profits at the end of the course. The best part of this course is that it's absolutely free. Unfortunately it's only offered periodically, which means that it's not always available.

The Build Emini Breakout Strategies Fast course is also offered by Nesnidal. This course consists of more than 20 educational videos and five modules that covers topics like the building blocks of a good breakout strategy, how to spot the right time to exit a trade, how to change your strategy as needed to match the current market conditions, how to apply a robustness test to your chosen breakout strategy, how to automate your breakout strategies, and how to make use of the system sizing approach. The main purpose of this course is to teach you how to pick financial securities like stocks or commodities that have moved outside of their ordinary support or resistance zones (called "breakout stocks" or "breakout commodities") and to help you to start seeing profits off of their trades right away. At only $297 for the entire course, it's well worth the money.

The Breakout Strategies Masterclass course is available at an additional fee to Better Systems Trader's students who have previously completed the Fourteen Day Breakout Strategy Challenge or the Build Emini Breakout Strategies Fast course. It builds on the knowledge that was shared during the aforementioned two courses by teaching its students about advanced robustness tests and how to apply Nesnidal's "Breakout Smart Code." If you are interested in completing this course, you should insure that you first complete the Fourteen Day Breakout Strategy Challenge or the Build Emini Breakout Strategies Fast course, after which you're encouraged to contact the Better System Trader's team to enquire about the cost of adding this course on to the one which you've already completed.

The Building Robust Trading Strategies Masterclass course is taught by Robert Pardo, an award-winning stockbroker, hedge fund manager, and the president of Pardo Capital Limited. Pardo is such a trading prodigy that he was named "Trader of the Year" in 2008 by *Futures* magazine. This course will teach you the importance of robustness, how to develop a successful and efficient trading strategy, how to optimize your trading strategy, how to determine your personal "optimization space," how to avoid overfitting, how to conduct a "Walk Forward" analysis, how to make use of Pardo's "Walk Forward Matrix" technique, how to make use of his "Big Leap" method, and how to monitor your securities portfolio in real-time. The Building Robust Trading Strategies Masterclass course contains hours upon hours' worth of educational content, covering even the little things like moving averages and giving you access to four of Prado's group coaching calls. Investing in this course will cost you just a little under $1,000 ($997, to be precise) although it is arguably worth the cost, as it has been incredibly well-reviewed by past students.

Better System Trader's Trading Market Internals course claims to be able to help you to reduce your losses and stock drawdowns by more than half. Fortunately you don't need to do much in order to be able to afford this valuable piece of education because it is entirely free. All it costs you is the time that it takes to enter your email address in order to have the course's material sent to you.

The Smashing False Breakouts course claims to be able to teach you a four-step process that is guaranteed to help you to invest in breakout financial securities by making it easier to spot them sooner and by teaching you how to recognize and avoid false breakouts. Just like the Trading Market Internals course, it is entirely free to complete and has no prerequisites in order for you to be able to finish it.

If you can't find anything up your alley among Better System Trader's courses, you should consider taking a gander at Investors Underground's educational offerings. Joining this wonderful community of stock traders and stockbrokers only costs about $297 per month (or $1,897 annually) and gives you access to a myriad of stock trading and day trading courses, the community's live chat room on which you can discuss current, past, and future trades, group webinars, an educational library full of free stock trading resources, and daily financial security watch lists covering everything from cryptocurrencies to forex and the stock market.

Of course if you're not tech-savvy enough to make use of an online course (or if you'd simply prefer not to pay for them), you could always head down to your local library to borrow some books on day trading. Rayner Teo, a successful trader and the owner of TradingWithRayner, believes that there are five books that all aspiring day traders absolutely have to read: *Market Wizards* by Jack Schwager, *Trend Following: Learn to Make Millions in Up or Down Markets* by Michael Covel, *The Complete Turtle Trader: How 23 Novice Investors Became Overnight Millionaires* by Michael Covel, *Technical Analysis of the Financial Markets: A Comprehensive Guide to Trading Methods and Applications* by John Murphy, and *Mind Over Markets: Power Trading with Market Generated Information* by James Dalton, Eric James, and Robert Dalton.

Market Wizards by Jack Schwager is a compilation of interviews with highly successful traders that the author conducted over a period of many years. Some of these traders managed to turn a few thousand dollars into millions, seemingly overnight, and they're more than happy to share their secrets and tips with Schwager's readers. Learning from the best is definitely one of the fastest routes to success, which is exactly what this book offers you.

Trend Following: Learn to Make Millions in Up or Down Markets by Michael Covel teaches its readers how to make use of Covel's trend following technique. He makes it easy to understand by providing a bunch of real world examples in which you can see this strategy in action. Learning how to spot long-term trends will help you to better be able to analyZe and predict short-term price movements (the kind that you'll aim to exploit as a day trader).

The Complete Turtle Trader: How 23 Novice Investors Became Overnight Millionaires by Michael Covel is like a day trader's spellbook. Owning it will help you to make magic. It tells the true story of a handful of rookie traders who were selected for a two-week study during which they were taught a number of proven trading strategies (that are also shared and elaborated in the book). It then traces their progress after completing the study and, lo and behold, many of them became millionaires in the blink of an eye, proving that all you need to become wealthy is a little bit of extra knowledge.

Technical Analysis of the Financial Markets: A Comprehensive Guide to Trading Methods and Applications by John Murphy aims to teach its readers the ins and outs of technical trading. It covers some more advanced technical analysis methods like candlestick charts and their interpretation and recognizing chart patterns. Both of these topics are really useful to budding day traders, but they need to be covered in depth to enable you to fully understand them (which Murphy does brilliantly). Having a clear understanding of the uses and applications of technical analysis will definitely help you to make better informed trades that result in higher profits.

Mind Over Markets: Power Trading with Market Generated Information by James Dalton, Eric James, and Robert Dalton teaches its readers how to make use of a revolutionary new stock chart interpretation technique called "market profiling." Market profiling allows you to predict whether stock prices will increase or decrease across the board on any particular trading day, which means that as a day trader you'll know whether it's a good day to execute a high volume of trades or not.

This book (the one you're reading right now) is a fantastic start, but you definitely shouldn't consider yourself fully educated on the topic of day trading by the time you reach the final page. Three hours might be enough time to get a grip on the basics of day trading, but you're going to need decades of dedication in order to become a master. If you make learning your goal, you'll soon find that your profits increase as your knowledge on the subject itself increases too. You should take care not to become overwhelmed by the sheer volume of day trading information out there; instead try to break it down into palatable chunks and research it in this way.

Chapter 5:

Psychology in the

Marketplace

"Psychology? Why do I need to know anything about psychology in order to work with numbers?" you might ask yourself, but the fact of the matter is that financial securities' prices are largely determined by how people feel about them. These "feelings" are called market psychology. The word "psychology" comes from the Greek word for soul (*psychē*) and the English suffix -ology, which is indicative of a field of study. In essence it is defined as being the study of human behaviors, thoughts, and motivations. Hundreds of economists and financial experts have dedicated decades of their lives to trying to understand it, but it remains somewhat elusive and poorly understood. The fact that we're still coming to grips with the human psyche and how it functions is absolutely extraordinary when you consider that human beings have been studying psychology and its implications since the middle of the ancient Egyptian and ancient Greek eras.

Why People's Feelings Can Drive a Stock's Price Up or Down

It seems counterintuitive that people's feelings are capable of driving the stock price of large companies like Apple or Amazon up or down. Yes, Susie down at the corner café's opinion on the company you've just invested in may affect the price you'll be able to sell the stocks you've just purchased. It's a terrifying concept, but it's something that you can learn to use to your advantage. A real world example of this phenomenon is when an oil company's stock price decreases after an oil spill out on the open ocean. The oil spill itself is unlikely to change a large oil company's financial position or profitability by much, but it will more than likely cause its stock price to plummet as investors condemn the resulting environmental damage.

The combined feelings that investors have towards a particular company and its stock is referred to as "market sentiment." Over the past couple of years more and more professional stockbrokers have started making use of market sentiment analysis in order to determine whether a stock's price is about to experience a short-term increase or decrease. They are able to do this by harnessing the power of market sentiment indicators. These indicators normally look at whether the majority of traders are holding a specific stock in long or short positions in order to determine the underlying market sentiment. The ratio of long positions to short positions generally indicates what traders' expectations of a specific company and its stock are, how the media has been portraying a specific company, and how traders feel about the service or product that the company is offering.

Other than considering a specific stock's long or short position ratio, market sentiment analysts also make use of put-to-call volume ratio, advance-decline ratio, new high to new low ratio, and the accumulation or distribution line.

A stock's put to call volume ratio can be used to determine its underlying market sentiment because the assumption can be made that traders investing in calls believe that the stock that they're investing in will increase in value over time while traders investing in puts probably think that the stock's price is about to experience a significant decrease. In other words it can be said that a stock's market sentiment is positive (meaning that its price is likely to experience an increase) when there are more traders who have invested in calls in it than there are traders who have invested in puts in it and vice versa.

Advance-decline ratios show how many shares belonging to a certain company are being bought (advanced) versus how many are being offered for sale (declined). Essentially this ratio is the measure of a stock's supply and demand. If more stocks are being bought than are being offered for sale, it's an indication that the stock's price is likely to start experiencing an increase while the opposite is true if more stocks belonging to a certain company are being offered for sale than are being bought.

New high to new low ratios show how often a stock sells for more than it ever previously has versus how often a stock sells for less than it ever previously has over a 52-week period. If a certain stock experiences more new highs (the highest price it has ever sold for) over the course of this period than it experiences new lows (the lowest price it has ever sold for), then its price is likely to experience a sustained increase. If a certain stock experiences more new lows than it experiences new highs over this period of time, then it is likely that its price will continue to experience a sustained downswing.

A stock's accumulation or distribution line is similar to its advance-decline ratio, with the main difference being that it shows the amount of stocks belonging to a certain company bought versus the number of stocks belonging to a certain company sold (instead of the number of stocks bought versus the number offered for sale). This relationship is also not represented in the form of a ratio; instead it is usually depicted as a line graph with its y-axis representing the number of publicly held shares and its x-axis representing a predetermined period of time (usually a year). Logically, if more stocks are being bought than are being sold, the stock's price will increase and vice versa.

If you don't feel up to doing all of the math or drawing up any corresponding charts in order to do market sentiment analysis, there are a number of useful market sentiment indicators that you could use instead, namely the CBOE Volatility Index (VIX), the NYSE High to Low Indicator, the NYSE 200-day Moving Average, Odd-Lot Trading Statistics, and the Commitment of Traders Report.

VIX is a value (usually a one- or two-digit number) that is given for stocks being traded on the Chicago Board of Options Exchange (abbreviated as CBOE); it is supposed to indicate whether a specific stock is going to experience an increase or decrease in value over the next 30 days. If this number is given in red, it means that the stock's price is predicted to decrease over the next 30 days. If it is given in green, it means that the stock's price is predicted to increase over the next 30 days. The CBOE calculates this value by considering a stock's volatility levels. Incredibly volatile stocks are predicted to devalue over a 30-day period while stocks that show very low levels of volatility are predicted to increase in value over a 30-day period.

The NYSE High to Low Indicator is a chart that is compiled by the NYSE itself. It shows the number of stocks being traded through it that are being sold versus the number of stocks being traded through it that are being bought. If more stocks are being bought through the NYSE than are being sold through the NYSE, this indicates that the market is bullish (which means that stocks are likely to be selling for more than they're actually worth). The inverse is true if more stocks are being sold through the NYSE than are being bought.

The NYSE 200-Day Moving Average is a percentage calculated by the NYSE itself that represents the number of stocks that are being traded through it that are selling for more than they were worth over the preceding 200-day period. The stock market is said to be generally bullish if more than half of the stocks that are available on the NYSE are selling for more than they were during the previous 200-day period while it is believed to be bearish if more than half of the stocks that are available on the NYSE are selling for less than they were during the previous 200-day period. It's important to know when the stock market is experiencing a bullish or bearish period, as sellers tend to be able to make more money during bullish periods while buyers are able to pick up better stocks during bearish periods.

Odd-Lot Trading Statistics are also represented as percentages. This percentage reflects the number of traders who are purchasing "odd lots." An odd lot is an amount of shares that is less than 100. Savvy traders know that they need to look out for an increase in the number of odd-lot trades being conducted in relation to the number of lot trades being conducted because when more odd-lot trades are being conducted than lot trades it indicates that more non-professionals are trading than professional stock traders are. While it's always wonderful to see new people getting involved in the stock market, it's certainly also concerning when professional stock traders and stockbrokers stop trading because it shows that they know something about the market that makes them believe that it is an inauspicious time to be conducting trades (even if you're perhaps entirely oblivious to this element). The reason why you can assume that odd lot trades are being conducted by nonprofessionals is that they're generally the only group of traders who might not have enough investment capital in order to buy a nice round lot of stocks.

The Commitment of Traders Report is a paper that is published every week that is made up of surveys pertaining to the level of speculative interest in futures held by traders. The more futures held in a certain stock, the more certain you can be that it's going to experience an increase in price. Of course, the inverse is also true.

Other than making use of some of the ratios and percentages mentioned above along with one or two of the aforementioned established market indicators, you can also get a feel for the market sentiment surrounding a specific stock by keeping abreast with market, local, national, and international news. If a drought is declared on national news, it might lead to negative market sentiment surrounding the outlook for agricultural companies, while a declaration of war might lead to positive market sentiment surrounding ammunition and arms producers.

The biggest problem with trading off of market sentiment indicators alone is that they don't give you a very good idea of the best time to enter or to exit trades. They simply vaguely indicate whether the stock's price is likely to increase or decrease at an unknown time in the future. You can circumvent any problems that might arise from this by making your trading decisions based on a number of analysis techniques, like technical or fundamental analysis alongside market sentiment analysis.

Protecting Your Own Psychological Well-Being While Day Trading

It would be absolutely pointless for you to know all of the secrets to successful day trading if your mental well-being will suffer despite it or if you're going to allow your mental state or emotions to negatively impact your trades. Stock trading, and consequently day trading, is largely a mental game that is fought, won, or lost inside of your mind. Learning to fortify your mind, to reign in your emotions, and to control your thoughts is an important, albeit lesser acknowledged, part of becoming a successful day trader.

Let me start off by saying that there are two emotions that all traders need to learn to compartmentalize when they're trading: greed and fear. Greed will lead you to buying stocks when you should be waiting to see what the market is going to do (or even when you're supposed to be selling instead) while fear will drive you to sell your financial securities when you should be holding on to them (or buying) instead. Traders tend to get greedy when they've experienced a prolonged period of profitable trades that lead them to believe they're incapable of failing. Unfortunately it is this confidence that often leads to their failure. In direct contrast to this, traders tend to become fearful when they've experienced a prolonged period of trades resulting in losses, and unfortunately this fear is often crippling, rendering them unable to make trading decisions effectively.

There are a number of techniques that you can utilize to better control your emotions although you first need to be able to recognize your emotions before you can learn how to tame them, this is best done by asking yourself what your motivations are for each trade that you are planning on performing. Psychologists suggest that once you've done this that you should be able to exercise a significant amount of control over your emotions by labeling them and then by reframing your thoughts. Labeling your emotions is as straightforward as examining what it is that you're feeling and giving it a name. For example, perhaps you've just lost a lot of money on a bad trade; that heavy feeling in your chest might be humiliation, disappointment, sadness, or anxiety. Labeling it as what it truly is will help you to complete the next step: reframing your thoughts.

Once you know what exactly it is that you're feeling, you can guide your mind to come to a more positive conclusion, one which you can actually grow from instead of just feeling bad about yourself. An example of this would be if you realize that you feel humiliated after losing a lot of money on a bad trade. This realization could be used to draw the conclusion that you're basing your sense of self-worth on your financial success and thus reframing your thoughts would involve realizing that you are worth much more than the contents of your bank account.

Stock traders are one of the groups of people that are notoriously prone to developing anxiety or depression because their chosen profession is inherently filled with a lot of uncertainty and numerous financial ups and downs. Losing money and then being unsure of when you'll be able to recover any of it (and if you'll ever be able to recover any of it) is enough to make even the most emotionally stable person crack on a bad day.

It's important to be able to spot the symptoms of anxiety and depression in yourself so that you can seek treatment if they become an undesirable side effect of your day trading career. Depression is generally characterized by a general feeling of numbness, sadness, guilt, or grief that lasts for a prolonged period of time and that may lead to changes in your weight and sleeping patterns. It can also lead to previously enjoyable activities becoming dull, boring, or just generally uninteresting and can negatively affect your concentration. Anxiety disorders are characterized by a general feeling of restlessness, worry, and stress that often leads to ordinary events feeling more stressful than they usually would. If you feel like you might be suffering from either anxiety or depression after you've been day trading full-time for a while, it's important that you seek out mental health resources like counseling, therapy, and medication, if need be.

Studies have shown that you can also keep anxiety or depression at bay, or at the very least, relieve the severity of their symptoms, by improving your diet, practicing mindfulness, getting enough exercise, and getting enough sleep. As an aspiring day trader you should make an effort to immunize yourself against mental health problems by:

- Following a healthy diet that eliminates, or at the very least reduces, your consumption of processed or sugary foods;
- Getting at least 30 minutes of exercise five times a week; whether it is in the form of a gym workout, a home workout, a walk, a jog, swimming, or horseback riding doesn't seem to matter, what is important is that you get moving;
- Getting between six and eight hours of sleep every night; and
- Practicing mindfulness techniques like meditation, controlled breathing, or yoga.

If you find yourself in a dark place and need to talk to someone about it, you should contact the National

Suicide Prevention Lifeline at 1-800-273-8255. If you are hard of hearing or suffer from social anxiety, you may prefer to get in contact with them through their online chat option at www.suicidepreventionlifeline.org/chat.

Chapter 6:

Strategy Is Everything

Wars have been won and lost because of effective (or defective) strategies, and day trading is no different. You need to be armed with a foolproof trading strategy if you want to spend next summer on your private yacht in the Bahamas.

If you're going into day trading and you're under the impression that you'll manage to make money by buying and selling with nothing but your intuition to guide you, you're in for a horrible wake-up call. If it was easy to be a billionaire, everyone would do it. Unfortunately you need to analyze, plot, scrutinize, and study every single stock that you're planning on investing in to make sure that it fits into your pre-existing trading strategy.

If you want to make the big bucks, your chosen day trading strategy should become your new mantra. You should eat it, sleep it, dream it, and immerse yourself in it entirely. You should tell your friends and family about it, you should write in your diary about it—it is absolutely imperative that it becomes as much a part of you as your DNA is.

What Are the Different Kinds of Day Trading Strategies?

So you're ready to swear fealty to your trading strategy? Well, hold your horses—you need to choose one before you can dedicate your life to it. There are three main day trading strategies: scalping, true day trading, and swing trading. Which one will be best-suited to you depends entirely on your needs and expectations.

Scalping might sound like a fate that would befall a cowboy in an old Western movie, but luckily it's a bit less brutal than that. This trading strategy involves buying hundreds (if not thousands) of shares and then selling them again soon thereafter to exploit an often miniscule difference in price. An example of this style of trading would be if you purchased 1,000 stocks of Apple at $318.22 per share and sold them again a few minutes later for $318.62 for a total of $400. Executing a single trade like this every day could see you earning as much as $12,400 every month for a few minutes of work every 24 hours. The main problem with this trading strategy is that it is largely inaccessible to beginner day traders because of the amount of investment capital that you need to pull it off. For example, you need $318,220 in order to buy 1,000 shares in Apple at $318.22 per share; that's a significant amount of money and a sum that you are unlikely to have simply lying around somewhere. Scalping without enough investment capital to enable you to buy hundreds or thousands of stocks at once is an exercise in futility because your profit margins will simply be too small for it to be a practical way of making money.

True day trading is exactly what its name suggests it to be: it's day trading. This strategy involves buying stocks at a lower price during the trading day only to sell them again for a higher price (if all goes well) before the trading day's end. The main difference between true day trading and scalping is that day traders tend to hold on to stocks for a couple of hours longer than scalpers do, and this means that they're able to exploit larger price differences. These larger differences in price mean that day traders don't need to buy nearly as many stocks as scalpers do in order to see a notable profit. An example of day trading would be buying 100 shares in McDonald's for $177 per share at 9am only to sell all of them again for $197 per share at 5pm, making a solid $2,000. If you executed only one trade like this every single day, you could potentially see a profit of $62,000 per month.

Swing trading, while often classified alongside day trading, actually entails holding onto a financial security for more than a single trading day. Some swing traders hold on to their chosen investments for more than a week before selling them again. The main benefit of swing trading is that you need even less initial investment capital for it than you do for day trading because the longer period of time between purchase and sale allows you to exploit even larger price differences. For example, if you bought 50 shares in a friend's start-up technology business called

ComputersRUs for $1.50 per share and a week later the company merged with Google, driving its stock price up to $60 per share, and you then sold all of the ComputersRUs shares that you initially purchased, you would make $2,925. If you conducted just one trade like this every week, your monthly income could be as much as $11,700.

You should choose a trading strategy based on the amount of time you're willing to put in, the amount of capital that you're capable of investing, and the kind of profits that you'd like to see. If you have quite a lot of time and money on your hands and you would like to regularly see some hefty profits, then scalping might be just the strategy for you. On the other hand, if you have a lot of time to invest but not a lot of money and you'd still like to see some impressive profits, then you should consider true day trading. If you have neither time nor money to throw at it, then you should take up swing trading.

There's not one particular trading strategy that is better than all of the rest; the best trading strategy is the one that suits your lifestyle and wallet.

How To Research Stocks

Regardless of the day trading strategy that you choose to use, it's important that you research all of the stocks that you invest in at least a little bit. Researching a stock and its holding company can give you a better idea of whether it is about to increase or decrease in value, and at the very least you should have an idea of the kind of business venture that you're supporting.

The very first thing that you need to dig up when you're trying to research a stock is its holding company's annual report. The SEC requires by law that all publicly traded companies submit a copy of their annual financial report to it at least once a year. A company's annual report contains information pertaining to its profitability, its financial and operational projections, its financial and operational aspirations, its debts, its liabilities, and any new innovations that it may be intent on revealing to the public soon. These days it's pretty easy to find a company's annual report because companies usually make them available to the public on their websites. If you can't find a company's annual report anywhere, you can always request it from them directly or you could search for it on annualreports.com, a website that hosts the annual reports of nearly all of America's publicly traded companies. Companies that are profitable and that have few debts tend to have higher stock prices that increase as the company's financial position improves while companies that are failing financially tend to have lower stock prices that decrease as the company's future prospects worsen.

There are also a number of mathematical values that can be used to determine whether a specific stock's price is liable to experience an upswing or a downswing, namely price-to-earnings ratios, price/earnings growth ratios, earnings per share, price-to-sales ratio, price-to-book ratio, dividend payout ratios, dividend yields, and returns on equity.

A stock's price-to-earnings ratio is calculated by taking the price that it is currently selling for and dividing it by the amount of money the company has made per share that it has issued. For example, if ComputersRUs made $100 000 in the previous fiscal year, has issued 100 shares in total, and is currently trading for $10 per share, then its price to earnings ratio would be $10:1,000 (or $1:100). A high price-to-earnings ratio indicates that the stock is currently selling for more than it is actually worth and that it will start to decrease in value soon. A low price-to-earnings ratio means that the stock is selling for less than it is really worth and that it will start to increase in value soon. If you're day trading, you always want to keep an eye out for stocks with low price-to-earnings ratios.

A stock's price/earnings growth ratio is believed to be an even better measure of a company's future prospects than its price-to-earnings ratio is, but you first need to calculate a company's price-to-earnings ratio before you'll be able to determine its price/earnings growth ratio, which is calculated by dividing its price-to-earnings ratio by its growth rate. This numerical value is of value to day traders because it can be used to determine when it's a good time to sell and which stocks are good investment options. Stocks with lower price/earnings growth ratios are likely to experience an imminent increase in price, which means that they're a good investment option for day traders while stocks with higher price/earnings growth ratios will probably decrease in value in the near future, which means that you should sell them before this starts to happen.

A stock's earnings per share value is used to determine the profitability of its holding company. As was mentioned earlier, profitable companies always have more expensive stocks. It's a relatively easy numerical value to calculate. All you need to do in order to extrapolate it is take a stock's holding company's overall profits and divide them by the amount of stocks that it has issued since it started trading publicly. Earnings per share values aren't used by day traders as often, as they're used by long-term investors because they are a better measure of a stock's long-term growth projections than they are of any imminent price changes that it might experience. Stocks with high earnings per share values are likely to continue increasing in price over a period of time while stocks with lower earnings per share values are in danger of decreasing in price.

A stock's price-to-sales ratio is also called its "revenue multiple" or its "sales multiple." It is a measure of the amount of money that a company makes from selling products or services when compared to the amount of stocks it has issued since it started trading publicly. Consequently, it is calculated by dividing a company's profit from sales by the amount of stocks it has and then dividing the price of one stock in the company by this value. Logically, this value can't be applied to publicly traded companies who do not make their money from the sale of products or services. If a stock has a low price to sales ratio, it indicates that it will more than likely experience an increase in price soon while the opposite is true if it has a high price to sales ratio.

Companies use their price-to-book ratio (also called price-to-equity ratio) to determine the difference between their value on the stock market and their real value (book value) that is calculated by subtracting their liabilities from their assets. They determine this ratio by dividing the price of a single one of their stocks by their book value per share (which is further extrapolated by dividing their book value by the number of shares that they've issued since they started trading publicly). Stock traders, and thus day traders, can make use of this ratio to determine whether a stock's price is likely to increase or decrease in the future. Stocks with a price-to-book ratio of less than one are likely to increase in value while stocks with a price-to-book ratio of one or more are likely to decrease in value. In other words, as a day trader you want to make sure that you invest in stocks with price-to-book ratios of less than one.

Dividend yield is a percentage that shows investors how much they can expect to get back for every dollar that they spend on stocks belonging to a certain company. For example, if ComputersRUs has a dividend yield of sixty percent, then you can expect to earn back $0.60 in dividends for every dollar that you spend on purchasing its stocks. Day traders don't often consider a stock's dividend yield when they're trying to decide which stocks to buy because it doesn't really create any short-term price changes on the stock market.

A stock's dividend payout ratio (also referred to as its payout ratio) is a value that stock traders use when they're trying to find out how much of its profits a company is sharing with its shareholders. Day traders aren't really concerned about companies' dividend payouts because they never hold on to stocks long enough in order to share in them, but knowing this value can be valuable nonetheless because you can use it to determine whether a stock is doing well or not. It is calculated by taking the amount of dividends paid out by a company over a fiscal year and dividing them by its profits over the course of that same fiscal year. Companies with higher dividend payout ratios tend to have more expensive stocks because they're more popular among investors (this increase in demand drives their prices up) while companies with lower dividend payout ratios tend to have less expensive stocks. It is important to note that a company's stock price tends to fall quite a bit directly after it has made dividend payouts to its stockholders. This occurs for two reasons—one monetary and one psychological. The first is because the dividend dilutes the stock's value. The second is because traders know that it'll be a while before it makes any dividend payouts again, which makes it a less attractive option for medium-term traders.

A stock's return on equity is used to determine how efficiently its holding company generates money for its shareholders. It is extrapolated by taking a stock's holding company's net income over a period of five years and dividing it by the amount of money shareholders spent on acquiring its shares over the same period. As is the case with dividend-based ratios and percentages, it isn't really applicable to day traders (although it is very valuable to long- and medium-term stock traders), but it can be used to determine whether a stock is experiencing a long-term downswing or a long-term upswing. Stocks that have high returns on equity are likely experiencing long-term upswings while stocks that have low returns on equity are in danger of experiencing downswings. Stocks that are experiencing long-term upswings are always a good choice for day traders.

Sounds complicated? It's really not, and it will become simpler and easier as you spend more time examining and studying these numerical values. Luckily you have other options when it comes to stock analysis and picking stocks if numbers aren't your thing—stock charts.

The best place to view stock charts is on Google Finance. They're entirely free and very accurate; all you need to do in order to access them is visit www.google.com/finance and enter into the search bar the stock's ticker whose chart you'd like to view. As a day trader, you'll usually be interested only in a stock's price movements over the course of a single trading day, so you'll select the "one day" option at the top of the chart. Another nifty aspect of Google Finance's stock charts is the fact that they also display the stock's open, high, low, market capitalization, price-to-earnings ratio, dividend yield, previous close, 52-week high, and 52-week low if and when these values are available.

For a day trader, the most important part of a stock chart is its trend line. The stock charts available on Google or Yahoo Finance are line charts, which means that their trend line is the only line that runs perpendicularly from the Y-axis (which indicates the stock's price). A stock's trend line shows the movements of its price over a predetermined period of time. In years gone by stock traders used this line to predict what the stock's price was likely to do next, but today most financial platforms (including Google Finance) do the predicting for you and reflect this prediction as a gray line extending from and continuing on the already existing trend line (that is normally either red or blue depending on the platform that you're using). This prediction will tell you whether a stock's price is likely to go up or down in the immediate future. If you're viewing a stock's one-day stock chart and you see that the prediction stemming from the trend line suddenly shoots upwards, then you should jump in and invest immediately as it's likely that the stock depicted will experience a significant increase in price at some point during the trading day.

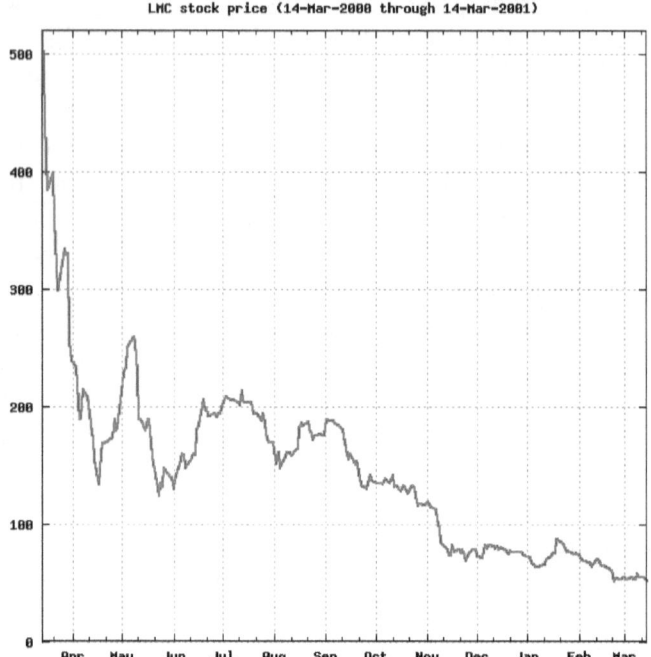

LMC stock price (14-Mar-2000 through 14-Mar-2001)

Some financial platforms, like Yahoo Finance (easily and freely accessible at finance.yahoo.com), also show you the stock's trading volume. This is usually shown at the bottom of the stock chart as a bunch of blue, red, or green bars. While it's not nearly as helpful to a day trader as a stock's trendline is, it can be used to analyze whether a stock's price is set to increase or decrease in the future, which can be used in conjunction with a stock's trend line data in making the choice on whether to add it to your day trading portfolio or not. If a stock's price steadily starts decreasing while its trading volume increases (either drastically or gradually), this could be a sign that investors have lost faith in it, which means that its price will likely continue to decrease over the long term. If a stock's price increases along with its trading volume, then it's a sure sign that it is in demand and that its price will likely continue to increase over the long term.

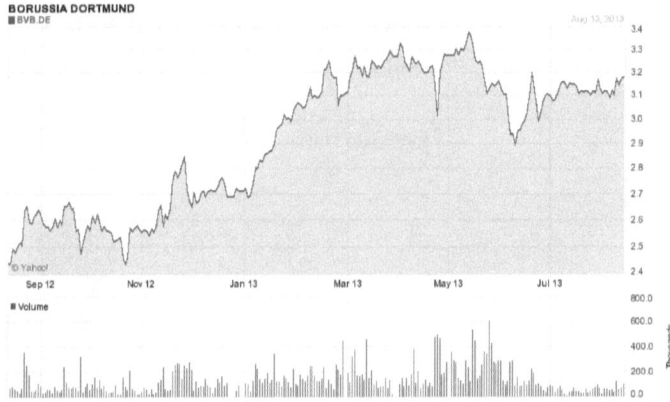

The third and final aspect of trading charts that you need to consider are their lines of support and resistance. Unfortunately, unlike trend lines and trading volume, these lines are not indicated on the chart itself and need to be plotted by the user themself. You can find a stock's resistance line by examining its trend line and determining the price point that it doesn't regularly increase above; this is its resistance point. Its resistance line is a theoretical horizontal line running straight between these resistance points. If a stock is currently trading at a price that is close to its resistance line, you can rightly assume that it's more likely to experience a price decrease next than it is to experience a price increase. Inversely, you can find a stock's support line by examining its trend line and determining the price point which it doesn't regularly decrease below; this is its support point (because it supports its price from falling any lower). Its support line is a theoretical horizontal line running straight between these support points. If a stock is currently trading at a price that is close to its support line, you can assume that it's more likely to experience an increase in price next than it is to experience a decrease in price.

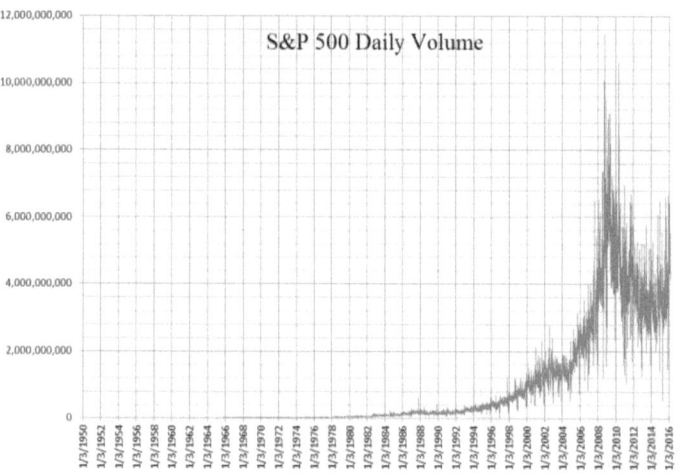

At the end of the day you can have all of the theoretical stock research and stock picking knowledge in the world, but the only way to truly hone your skills and gain the ability to spot a winner every time comes from practice. Lots and lots of practice. You'll likely bump your head a few times and choose a couple of losers, but it's all part of the process. You'll be able to smell a money-maker a mile off in no time and you'll look fondly back at this point in time, back when stock charts used to be confusing.

Conclusion

Well, now you know the basics and you should be well on your way to making millions and living the kind of life you've always dreamed of living, but where to start?

First you need to save up some investment capital if you don't have some squirrelled away already. As I discussed in chapter two, the amount of initial investment capital that you need depends on the kind of financial security that you'd like to start trading; stocks are the most expensive while cryptocurrency and forex are your cheaper options (although this doesn't mean that they're necessarily any less profitable).

Next you'll want to set up a demo-account to test your day trading skills before you invest (and possibly lose) any real money. I recommended a bunch of great demo-account platforms in chapter three, any of which would be a fantastic place to start. You should spend at least six weeks trading with your demo-account every day before you open a real trading account; some professional day traders even recommend sticking with a demo-account for up to six months before switching over to the real thing.

During this time period you should also settle on a trading strategy that you feel suits you best; it should also be one that you're able to trade well with. You should experiment with a couple of day trading, swing trading, and scalping strategies for a while before making your choice to ensure that it is suitable in practice and not just in theory. You might like the concept of being a scalper when you're actually a far better swing trader. Testing out as many strategies as possible will give you an honest insight into your skillset and the strategy that is most compatible with it.

Once you're consistently making profits on your demo-account, you should open a trading account through a brokerage firm. I named a myriad of brilliant firms in chapter three, although you should shop around a bit to find out who has the best rates and advisors before making your choice.

As soon as you've opened a trading account, it's time to start trading. Remember to make use of some of the skills pertaining to market sentiment analysis and researching stocks that were taught in chapters five and six before investing in any financial securities. It's important that you make your stock, commodity, forex, and cryptocurrency picks based on data rather than just a gut feeling. We all have gut feelings, but not everybody knows how to properly research stocks. This is why everybody is capable of day trading, but not everybody manages to make millions doing it.

That's really all there is to it: save up, demo-account, real account, and you've started your day trading career. Quite simple, isn't it?

The truth is that day trading isn't complicated, it's easy. This means that everybody is capable of making a living from doing it, including you. I know that if you set your mind to it, if you really dedicate yourself heart and soul to it, you'll be the next stock market millionaire. You've already proven that you have the will to do it by reading this book, and that's ninety percent of the battle won already. I can't wait to read your name headlining an article on financial success in *Forbes* or *Finweek*.

I mean, doesn't everybody who is willing to work for it deserve financial freedom? If you think so, why don't you leave a review on this book telling us what your financial goals are. Then you'll have something to reflect back on in a couple of years' time when you're one of the nation's most successful day traders. You could even quote it in your future autobiography.

References

An Introduction to Day Trading. (2019). Investopedia. https://www.investopedia.com/articles/trading/05/011705.asp

Andrew Beattie. (n.d.). 5 Skills That Traders Need. Investopedia. https://www.investopedia.com/articles/investing/091714/5-skills-traders-need.asp

Barrels of Oil. (n.d.). In Needpix.com. https://storage.needpix.com/rsynced_images/drums-1132226_1280.jpg

Bear Bull Traders | Learning Community of Serious Traders. (n.d.). https://www.benzinga.com/go/bear-bull-traders-trading-chatrooms/

Better System Trader Day Trading Courses. (n.d.). Better System Trader. http://bettersystemtrader.com/

Bitcoin. (n.d.). In Pikist.com. https://p0.pikist.com/photos/800/316/finance-currency-bitcoin-crypto-cryptocurrency-investment-wealth-money.jpg

Bull and Bear. (n.d.). In Pixabay.com. https://cdn.pixabay.com/photo/2015/02/20/06/19/stock-exchange-642896_960_720.jpg

Bulls on Wall Street | Day Trading | Swing Trading | Learn To Trade Stocks. (n.d.). Bulls on Wall Street. https://bullsonwallstreet.com/

Burning Money. (n.d.). In Wallpaperflare.com. https://c0.wallpaperflare.com/preview/161/585/207/burned-100-us-dollar-banknotes.jpg

Celebrating. (n.d.). In Pxfuel.com. https://p0.pxfuel.com/preview/405/830/467/achievement-african-bridge-business.jpg

Chicago Board of Options Exchange CBOE. (n.d.). In Flickr.com. https://live.staticflickr.com/2325/2534200127_d7cb69de31_b.jpg

Day trading. (2020, May 23). Wikipedia. https://en.wikipedia.org/wiki/Day_trading

Day Trading 101: How To Day Trade Stocks for Passive Income. (n.d.). Udemy. https://www.benzinga.com/go/day-trading-101-how-to-day-trade-stocks-for-passive-income/

Day Trading 2020 How to Start for Beginners - Tutorials and Strategies. (n.d.).

Www.Daytrading.Com.
https://www.daytrading.com/

Day Trading Advantages - Flexible Hours, Trade Stocks from Home, More. (n.d.). JobMonkey. https://www.jobmonkey.com/daytrading/adva ntages/

Day Trading Courses | Online Training & In Person Seminars. (n.d.). Warrior Trading. https://www.benzinga.com/go/warrior-trading-course-specific/

Day Trading Cryptocurrency: Crypto Trading Strategies 101. (2018, May 7). BitDegree Tutorials. https://www.bitdegree.org/tutorials/day-trading-cryptocurrency

Day Trading in the Commodities Markets. (n.d.). Dummies. https://www.dummies.com/personal-finance/investing/day-trading/day-trading-in-the-commodities-markets

Day Trading Options. (2020). Daytrading.Com. https://www.daytrading.com/options

Day Trading Strategies. (n.d.). The Balance. https://www.thebalance.com/day-trading-strategies-4073425

Day Trading Strategies - For Beginners To Advanced Day Traders, Strategy is Key. (n.d.).

Www.Daytrading.Com.
https://www.daytrading.com/strategies

Day Trading Terminology - 35 Terms You Should
Know. (2015, December 30). SpeedTrader.
https://speedtrader.com/35-day-trading-terms-
you-should-be-aware-of

Depression. (n.d.). In Flickr.com.
https://live.staticflickr.com/7378/13974181800
_649e6e5ae9_b.jpg

Dictionary Reference. (n.d.). In pxhere.com.
https://c.pxhere.com/photos/9f/cb/dictionary
_reference_book_learning_meaning_knowledge
_text_education_information-535832.jpg!d

Dow Jones Industrial Average. (n.d.). In Wikimedia
Commons.
https://upload.wikimedia.org/wikipedia/comm
ons/thumb/c/cf/Dow_Jones_Industrial_Avera
ge.svg/750px-
Dow_Jones_Industrial_Average.svg.png

Female Hand Holding Cocktail. (n.d.). In pxhere.com.
https://c.pxhere.com/photos/85/2f/female_h
and_holding_cocktail_glass_big_beverage_cold-
885734.jpg!d

Forex. (n.d.). In Pxfuel.com.
https://p1.pxfuel.com/preview/845/461/100/
chart-trading-courses-forex.jpg

40 Key "Stock Trading Terms For Beginners" Tips {INFOGRAPHIC}. (2019, January 5). StocksToTrade.Com. https://stockstotrade.com/40-trading-terms-beginners-infographic/

4 Strategies that Will Make you a Professional Day Trader. (n.d.). Udemy. https://www.benzinga.com/go/4-strategies-that-will-make-you-a-professional-day-trader-from-udemy/

Glossary of Stock Market Terms & Definitions. (2018). Nasdaq.Com. https://www.nasdaq.com/glossary

Graduation Ceremony. (n.d.). In Wallpaperflare.com. https://c1.wallpaperflare.com/preview/376/837/86/graduation-people-ceremony-diploma.jpg

Hands Holding Money. (n.d.). In pxfuel.com. https://p1.pxfuel.com/preview/441/29/76/money-donation-donate-profit.jpg

How Can I Learn Day Trading? (n.d.). MagnifyMoney. https://www.magnifymoney.com/blog/investing/day-trading/

How to Become a Day Trader - Day Trading Psychology. (2019, November 1). The Trader Chick. https://thetraderchick.com/day-trader-psychology/

How to Start Day Trading | Wealthsimple. (2015). @wealthsimple. https://www.wealthsimple.com/en-us/learn/how-to-start-day-trading#what_is_day_trading

Investing 101: How To Read A Stock Chart For Beginners. (n.d.). Money Under 30. https://www.moneyunder30.com/how-to-read-a-stock-chart

Investor's Business Daily. (2020, May 22). Stock Chart Reading For Beginners: What's In A Chart? Why Use Charts? Investor's Business Daily. https://www.investors.com/how-to-invest/stock-chart-reading-for-beginners/

Investors Underground - Day Trading Courses. (n.d.). Investors Underground. https://www.investorsunderground.com/

Lewis, M. (n.d.). What Is Day Trading for a Living - Benefits & Risks. Money Crashers. https://www.moneycrashers.com/what-is-day-trading/

Market Rebellion Courses. (n.d.). Marketrebellion.Com. https://www.benzinga.com/go/market-rebellion-day-trading/

NASDAQ. (n.d.). In Wikimedia Commons. https://upload.wikimedia.org/wikipedia/comm

ons/6/66/NASDAQ_stock_market_display.jpg

Piggy Bank. (n.d.). In Pexels.com. https://images.pexels.com/photos/9660/business-money-pink-coins.jpg?cs=srgb&dl=money-pink-coins-pig-9660.jpg&fm=jpg

Pile of Money. (n.d.). In Pixabay.com. https://cdn.pixabay.com/photo/2014/10/23/10/10/dollar-499481_960_720.jpg

Royal, J. (n.d.). Best Online Brokers For Day Trading In June 2020. Bankrate. https://www.bankrate.com/investing/best-online-brokers-for-day-trading/

Running to Money. (n.d.). In Piqsels.com. https://p0.piqsels.com/preview/763/518/414/chasing-money-run.jpg

Special Offers on Courses - Investors.com. (n.d.). Shop.Investors.Com. https://www.benzinga.com/go/investors-business-daily/

Sraders, A. (n.d.). How to Read Stocks: Charts, Basics and What to Look For. TheStreet. https://www.thestreet.com/how-to/read-stocks-14948162

Start Line. (n.d.). In Flickr.com. https://encrypted-tbn0.gstatic.com/images?q=tbn%3AANd9GcS

xeFagTWPZbLJZbrITU2A4lmJPJD-
jSWE01RbWtpNIeO7S-qHh&usqp=CAU

Stock Market Glossary | Stock Trading Terms
Dictionary. (n.d.). Www.Firstrade.Com.
https://www.firstrade.com/content/en-
us/education/glossary

Stock Chart. (n.d.). In *Publicdomainpictures.net*.
https://www.publicdomainpictures.net/picture
s/280000/nahled/chart-graph.jpg

Trade Volume. (n.d.). In *Wikimedia Commons*.
https://upload.wikimedia.org/wikipedia/comm
ons/5/58/S_and_P_500_daily_volume_chart_
1950_to_2016.png

10 Day Trading Strategies for Beginners. (2019).
Investopedia.
https://www.investopedia.com/articles/trading
/06/daytradingretail.asp

The Complete Day Trading Course (Updated 2020).
(n.d.). Udemy.
https://www.benzinga.com/go/the-complete-
day-trading-course-from-udemy/

37 Stock Trading Terms Every Trader Needs to Know.
(2019, January 3). Timothy Sykes.
https://www.timothysykes.com/blog/trading-
terms-you-need-to-know/

Trading Psychology – 11 Things that Separate Winners from Losers. (2019, March 21). - Tradingsim. https://tradingsim.com/blog/trading-psychology/

Trading Psychology: How to Get Into the Mindset of a Successful Trader. (2018, February 28). Timothy Sykes. https://www.timothysykes.com/blog/improve-trading-psychology/

Trading Psychology Tips & Tricks that Actually Work | Day Trading Forex Live – Advanced Forex Bank Trading Strategies. (n.d.). Www.Daytradingforexlive.Com. https://www.daytradingforexlive.com/trading-psychology-tips-tricks-that-actually-work/

Trading Without a Broker. (n.d.). Do It Right. https://www.ally.com/do-it-right/investing/trading-without-a-broker/

What Is Day Trading and Should You Do It? (2019, February 12). The Ascent. https://www.fool.com/the-ascent/buying-stocks/articles/what-is-day-trading-should-you-do-it/

What is Forex Day Trading? (n.d.). Admiral Markets (United Kingdom). https://admiralmarkets.com/education/articles/forex-basics/forex-day-trading-

explained#:~:text=Day%20trading%20is%20a
%20trading